CW00469788

DEVONSHIRE RAILWAYS

DEVONSHIRE RAILWAYS

COLIN G. MAGGS

HALSGROVE

Acknowledgement

I would like to thank Colin Roberts sincerely for
checking and improving the text.

First published in Great Britain in 2010

British Library Cataloguing-in-Publication Data
A CIP record for this title is available from the British Library

ISBN 978 1 84114 912 7

HALSGROVE
Halsgrove House,
Ryelands Industrial Estate,
Bagley Road, Wellington, Somerset TA21 9PZ
Tel: 01823 653777   Fax: 01823 216796
email: sales@halsgrove.com

Part of the Halsgrove group of companies
Information on all Halsgrove titles is available at: www.halsgrove.com

Printed and bound by The Cromwell Press Group, Wiltshire

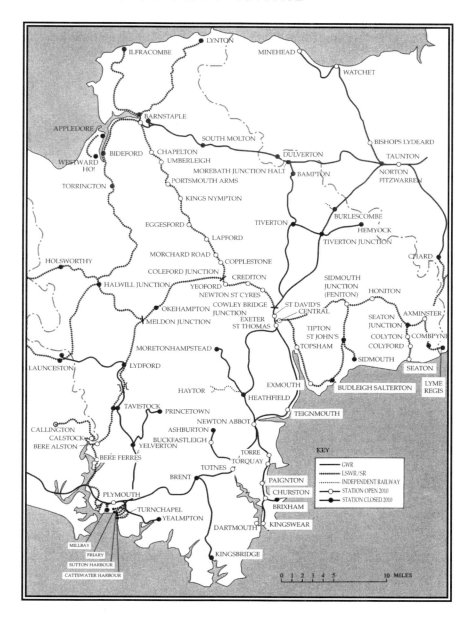

Contents

1 An Outline Survey of Railways in Devonshire

DEVON'S FIRST railway was opened as long ago as 16 September 1820. This was the Haytor Tramway constructed by George Templar and designed to expedite the carriage of granite from Haytor to a point north of Teigngrace where the stone was transhipped to a barge on the Stover Canal and carried to a sea-going vessel at Teignmouth.

Rather than using iron or timber rails like its contemporary British railways, the Haytor Tramway used the material readily available – granite. This material had the additional advantage that it was stronger than the alternatives, for cast iron rails broke all too easily. The granite blocks were

carved to form a flange on the inside and set to a gauge of four feet. The wagons were approximately 13ft in length and had four flangeless wheels two feet in diameter set loosely on axles. Traction was supplied by horses and as the line descended 1200ft in nine miles, effort was only required on the empty return journey. The tramway fell out of use in 1858 when granite was obtained from cheaper sources elsewhere.

Sections of the tramway are still extant and scheduled as an Ancient Monument. The Haytor Vale to Manaton road crosses the tramway at the Ordnance Survey grid reference SX 769776 and about half a mile to the west can be seen some granite points.

The later railway map of Devon appears complicated, but is easier to comprehend when the history of the lines is understood. Basically two competing main lines thrust westwards to Plymouth – the Great Western Railway (GWR) and the London & South Western Railway (LSWR). As far as Exeter the GWR ran to the north of the LSWR, but west of that city the positions were reversed. South-east Devon, generally known as 'East Devon', was LSWR territory, South-west Devon, known as 'South Devon' was mostly GWR territory, while most of North Devon came under the LSWR's sphere. Partly due to its topography, Devon had an unusually large number of branch lines.

The broad gauge South Devon Railway 4-4-0ST *Zebra* at Torre 1870. It was built in 1866 and withdrawn at the gauge conversion May 1892. Author's collection

The first main line in the county was the broad gauge Bristol & Exeter Railway (B&E). This was extended to Plymouth by the South Devon Railway (SDR) and entailed two severe inclines and a length between Dawlish and Teignmouth beside the sea where the sea did, and does try to wash away the railway. The LSWR more sensibly kept away from the sea and served watering places in East Devon by short branches, in fact one of them, that to Exmouth, is still very much open and is a useful commuter line. Exeter St David's station where the railway runs north to south, has the interesting phenomenon that trains to Plymouth ran in opposite directions depending on their route: GWR trains to Plymouth ran south, while those of the LSWR ran north.

The county was involved in the gauge question. The B&E and the SDR, lines closely associated with the GWR and eventually taken over by that company, favoured the broad gauge of 7ft 0¼ in, whereas the LSWR

A broad gauge Rover class 4-2-2 passes Stoke Canon May 1891 hauling a Down express over mixed gauge track. The platforms are staggered either side of the level crossing. The station closed 1 July 1894 and was replaced by one 500yd to the south and sited immediately before the junction of the Exe Valley branch. The exceptionally tall signal has its coloured 'spectacles' lower down the post. Author's collection

employed the standard gauge of 4ft 8½ in. Although having two gauges prevented through running of rolling stock and thus created problems at stations where the two gauges met, the GWR knew that one advantage of retaining the broad gauge was that it deterred the LSWR from seeking running powers. Eventually the cost and inconvenience of transhipment at the break of gauge caused broad gauge lines to be converted and the last of this works was carried out in May 1892. From that month it meant that if one route between London, Exeter and Plymouth was blocked through accident, flood, landslip, or storm, trains could use the alternative route.

Although the LSWR was generally a standard gauge line, in Devon it also owned broad gauge. Shares in the broad gauge Exeter & Crediton Railway

Gauge conversion taking place at Plymouth Millbay, 6.00pm 21 May 1892. Author's collection

The first Up standard gauge Flying Dutchman leaves Plymouth Millbay 8.35am 23 May 1892 hauled by a 4-4-0T. It carries the express headcode of the day. Most of the track is on longitudinal sleepers. The goods shed stands on the right. Author's collection

were craftily purchased and the line converted to standard gauge. Then the Taw Vale Extension Railway from Crediton to Barnstaple (later renamed the North Devon & Dock Company), was opened on the broad gauge, so one road of the Exeter & Crediton was reconverted to broad gauge to carry trains to Exeter. The broad gauge trains from Crediton to Bideford were withdrawn 30 April 1877 and those between Exeter and Crediton 20 May 1892. The LSWR's successor, The Southern Railway, (SR), owned a narrow gauge line, the 1ft 11½ in Lynton & Barnstaple Railway.

Building a standard gauge line over the hilly and lightly populated terrain would have been uneconomic, but adopting the narrow gauge allowed curves to be much sharper and so the line could easily follow the contours. The SR purchased the independent line in March 1923, but despite improvements found that it could not compete with road traffic and so the line was closed in 1935. 19½ miles in length, it was the first major closure in Devon. It was regrettable that this highly scenic line shut, because had it lasted another twenty years it would have been an early candidate for preservation. Fortunately some of the trackbed became available and a length from Woody Bay station has been reopened and further extension planned.

Although many branch lines in Devon were closed either immediately following, or before the 1963 Beeching

Seal of the North Devon Railway & Dock Company. Author's collection

Report on Railways, some have reopened as preserved lines: Totnes to Buckfast; Paignton to Kingswear and the Plym Valley Railway. Much of the Seaton branch was relaid as a 2ft 9in gauge electric tramway. Some stations too have been reopened: Sidmouth Junction has opened as Feniton; Ivybridge, closed to passengers 2 March 1959, reopened 15 July 1994 as a park and ride station to reduce traffic to and from Plymouth, while Tiverton Junction moved to Tiverton Parkway to give improved road access.

Apart from the main railway companies, Devon possessed an independent standard gauge line, probably unique in having an exclamation mark in its name, the Bideford, Westward Ho! & Appledore Railway.

There were several locomotive-worked industrial lines including the standard gauge Devon Basalt & Granite Co near Christow, the Devon County Council's 2ft gauge quarry lines at Beacon Down, Parracombe and Wilminstone, Tavistock. Devon Great Consols Ltd, Tavistock, owned a 4½ mile long line, while the 7 mile long Lee Moor Tramway ran between Lee Moor and Plymouth. The Ivybridge China Clay Co Ltd had 7 miles of 3ft gauge track, while Devonport Dockyard worked a two mile long system and operated regular workmen's trains. The North Devon Clay Co Ltd owned the 3ft gauge Marland Light Railway to convey clay to Torrington station, but 4½ miles of the route was converted to form the standard gauge North Devon & Cornwall Light Railway, subsequently the narrow gauge only taking clay from mines to the works. The Westleigh Stone & Lime Co Ltd owned a ¾ mile long 3ft gauge line between the quarry and the broad gauge Burlescombe station.

A significant amount of passenger and freight traffic in Devonshire was transient, passing through the county from the North, Bristol and London, to or from Cornwall. Often on summer Saturdays, holiday traffic was so dense that as soon as one train left a section, another entered. The principal expresses passing through Devon on the Western Region (WR) of British Railways (BR) were: the Cornish Riviera Limited, The Cornishman, The Devonian, The Golden Hind, the Mayflower, the Royal Duchy and the Torbay Express, while the Southern Region (SR) ran the Atlantic Coast Express and the Devon Belle, the latter a Pullman train with observation car at the rear.

Exeter and Plymouth were the two main railway centres in the county. In 1947 the GW shed at Exeter was allocated 34 locomotives, while the SR had 125 at Exmouth Junction. At Plymouth the numbers were 104 and 19 respectively. Newton Abbot was an important locomotive depot providing engines for the Torbay branch as well as assistant engines for hauling trains over the steep gradients to Plymouth. It had 73 locomotives in 1947. In the north of the county the SR stabled 14 at Barnstaple and the GWR 2.

2 How a Railway was Created

IN THE 19th century, businessmen and landowners wishing to improve trade, increase the value of their property and invest their cash profitably, might propose a scheme for linking two places by a railway. The way they went about such a scheme followed a general pattern which can be described once and serve to tell the story of the creation of almost any railway in Devon. Several meetings would be called in the locality and provided that sufficient financial support was promised, a bill would be placed before Parliament, itself often proving an expensive process. Committees of the houses of

NOTICE.
Culm Valley Light Railway.

ON

Monday next, Jan. 6, 1873,

At Half-past Two o'clock,

A MEETING

WILL BE HELD AT THE

STAR HOTEL HEMYOCK,

To receive a Report from the Directors of the above Company.

All Persons interested in the formation of this Railway are respectfully invited to attend.

Frederick Pollard,

SECRETARY,

Dated January 1st, 1873.   1, Upper Paul Street, Exeter.

Notice calling a meeting of the Culm Valley Light Railway 6 January 1873. Author's collection

11

Cutting the first
sod of the
Dartmouth &
Torquay Railway at
Torre 21 January
1858. Author's
collection

Commons and Lords received evidence for and against the proposed line. If both houses passed the bill it became an Act of Parliament and the promoting company was then legally entitled to raise a stipulated sum of money to purchase land and build the railway between the two chosen places. Before going to Parliament a surveyor would have drawn up plans. Ideally, a line would be straight, level, and pass through or close to chief settlements, yet using cheaper, rather than expensive land. If tunnels, cuttings and embankments were required, the surveyor would endeavour to make sure that soil excavated could be used in a nearby embankment. These plans, known as Deposited Plans, were placed with the local authority and Parliament. After the passing of the Act, with at least some of the capital raised, a contractor had to be found to carry out the work; those companies with less money would seek a contractor willing to work for shares rather than for cash.

Work usually began with the ceremonial turning of the first turf, a highly decorated spade being used to lift a sod into an equally ornate wheelbarrow. This was often done by the company's chairman or his wife. After the ceremony the directors and local dignitaries dined. The contractor set to work and was likely to meet difficulties – shortage of workers or materials, hard rock in an unexpected place that had to be cut through, or fluid clay that refused to stay in place. As a railway company might be unable to raise enough money to pay the contractor, or the contractor himself might go bankrupt, Parliament wisely decided that a railway company must deposit a sum of money, so that in the event of failure to complete the line after work had started, those funds deposited could be used to re-instate the property purchased compulsorily from the landowners. The Act of Parliament

stipulated that a line should be completed within a certain period of time and quite often, because of various difficulties, the railway was forced to apply to Parliament for an extension of time and not infrequently for an increase in capital to cover unforeseen costs.

When the contractor completed the line and before it could be opened to passenger traffic, an inspection had to be undertaken for the Board of Trade through an officer of the Royal Engineers. He went over the line testing bridge and other structures, making sure that the signalling was adequate for safety and the stations had suitable facilities. Usually at least one fault was discovered. If it was minor the Board of Trade granted a certificate subject to its correction; but in the event of a major criticism, re-inspection was required before the line could be opened.

On the opening day the directors and local dignitaries travelled over the line, dining afterwards. If the railway was a local one, it was usually worked by a larger company to make the business more economic. That was because,

Constructing the North Devon & Cornwall Junction Light Railway circa 1923. The lorry may well have been obtained from the WW1 Surplus Vehicles Disposal Sales at Slough. Author's collection

The arrival of the first train at Barnstaple on the opening of the North Devon Railway 12 July 1854. Notice the temporary grandstand on the right. Author's collection

The triumphal arch at Barnstaple for the opening of the NDR. Author's collection

Opening the South Devon & Tavistock Railway: the scene at Tavistock 22 June 1859. Author's collection

The first train headed by two locomotives arrives at Exmouth, 1 May 1861. Author's collection

although perhaps the line might require only one engine and two passenger coaches to work normal services, at least one more engine would be needed as a spare when the other engine was having a boiler wash-out or undergoing repair. On market days, fair days and Bank Holidays two coaches might prove insufficient. Some goods traffic required special rolling stock and it would be uneconomic to invest capital in something used only occasionally. To obviate such difficulties a small company therefore usually arranged for a larger company with larger resources to work the line for a percentage of the gross receipts. Some lines were far from profitable, ordinary shareholders rarely or never receiving a dividend, and it often happened that eventually a small railway was purchased by the working company, the payment usually less than its building cost.

In the early 1900s rail motors came into use. A rail motor was a passenger coach and locomotive contained on the same underframe. It was designed so that when going boiler-first the engine would be at the front, but when returning the driver could walk to what had been the rear and drive from a special control compartment, the fireman remaining at the other end. The use of a rail motor obviated the time and trouble needed to run an engine round its train at the end of every journey. When a rail motor service was introduced, unmanned halts were opened at places where traffic was insufficient to warrant a staffed station.

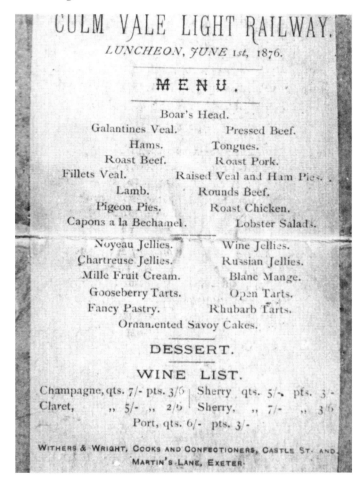

CULM VALE LIGHT RAILWAY.

LUNCHEON, JUNE 1st, 1876.

MENU.

Boar's Head.

Galantines Veal.   Pressed Beef.
Hams.   Tongues.
Roast Beef.   Roast Pork.
Fillets Veal.   Raised Veal and Ham Pies.
Lamb.   Rounds Beef.
Pigeon Pies.   Roast Chicken.
Capons a la Bechamel.   Lobster Salads.

Noyeau Jellies.   Wine Jellies.
Chartreuse Jellies.   Russian Jellies.
Mille Fruit Cream.   Blanc Mange.
Gooseberry Tarts.   Open Tarts.
Fancy Pastry.   Rhubarb Tarts.
Ornamented Savoy Cakes.

DESSERT.

WINE LIST.

Champagne, qts. 7/- pts. 3/6 | Sherry qts. 5/- pts. 3/-
Claret,   ,, 5/- ,, 2/6 | Sherry,   ,, 7/-   ,, 3/6
Port, qts. 6/- pts. 3/-

WITHERS & WRIGHT, COOKS AND CONFECTIONERS, CASTLE ST. AND MARTIN'S LANE, EXETER.

Menu for the luncheon given in the marquee, Hemyock, to celebrate the opening of the Culm Valley Light Railway. Author's collection

Rear view of a
steam rail motor
propelling a trailer
to Yealmpton as it
leaves Steer Point.
Author's collection

Seal of the Torbay
& Brixham
Railway opened in
1868 and sold to
the GWR in 1883.
Author's collection

Rail motors were found to
lack flexibility. If, on (say) a
market day, the number of
passengers quadrupled, a rail
motor could not cope as it was
only powerful enough to draw
one trailer. As a railway therefore required a locomotive and
coaches standing by for such
an eventuality, any saving
made by the rail motor was
lost.

The solution was a push-pull or auto train. An engine stayed at one end
of the train and on the return journey, the driver could control his engine
from a special compartment at what had been the rear by means of
mechanical rods or compressed air.

The year 1923 brought Grouping when, apart from very minor lines, all
railway companies became part of one of the Big Four: The Great Western
Railway, the London, Midland & Scottish Railway (LMS); the London &
North Eastern Railway (LNER) and the Southern Railway (SR). The GWR
was the only railway to retain its old name, the London & South Western
Railway becoming part of the SR. With Nationalisation on 1 January 1948
the GWR became British Railways Western Region, and the SR the Southern
Region , though minor area changes were made.

Railways were quick to spot the bus competitor and themselves
participated in road transport. Although the Lynton & Barnstaple Railway
did not itself run a bus service, its chairman Sir George Newnes formed the
Ilfracombe Motor Coach Company to operate a feeder service between

Blackmoor station and Ilfracombe using two Milnes-Daimler wagonettes. Inaugurated on 16 May 1903 it ceased in July when a driver was fined three pounds for exceeding 8mph. On 1 June 1903 two Milnes-Daimler LSWR buses began an Exeter, Queen Street to Chagford service. In 1905 they were replaced by Clarkson steam buses. Although the GWR owned its first bus in 1903, the first service in Devon ran between Brixton Road station Yealmpton and Modbury on 2 May 1905.

From 1928 legislation permitted railways to purchase large, but not controlling, shareholdings in existing bus companies. The GWR and SR reached agreement with the National Omnibus & Transport Company: the Western National was set up to run bus services in GWR territory, the railway agreeing to transfer its road motor services to that company in return for a half share, the Western National undertaking to co-ordinate rail and road services and not to compete with the railway. The Southern National operated similar services in the SR area.

In addition to bus competition, the increase in private car ownership in the 1950s and 1960s was another reason for the decline in the number of rail passengers and many of the poorly-frequented stations closed. The smaller stations remaining open were generally unstaffed, passengers purchasing their tickets from the conductor-guard on the diesel multiple unit pay trains. Freight traffic also declined because of increased use of road vehicles, especially at times when railwaymen were on strike, their actions permanently damaging business. The swing to the use of electricity, North Sea gas and oil for heating brought a decrease in the once very heavy coal traffic to almost every station. Fifty years ago railways carried relatively small loads to a variety of destinations; today the railways are mainly bulk carriers of stone, steel, cars, coal and oil.

GWR AEC bus No 228 at Kingsbridge 17 March 1925. This 45hp vehicle entered service 4 November 1919. Author's collection

3 Broad Gauge Lines: The Bristol & Exeter Railway

Burlescombe
station view Down
circa 1935. A
goods train emerges
from the Up loop
which gave access
to the quarry line.
Author's collection

ALMOST AS soon as the Act of Parliament had been passed in 1835 granting the Great Western Railway powers to build a line between Bristol and London, a prospectus was issued for creating an extension to Exeter. No time was lost. Within a month the estimated capital of £1½ m had been subscribed, a survey made and the necessary plans deposited. The GWR and the B&E shared the same engineer, I.K.Brunel and both railways were built to the broad gauge.

Although the line to Beam Bridge, west of Wellington, was opened on 1 May 1843, Whiteball Tunnel was incomplete and needed another year's work,

so stage coaches carried passengers from the eight daily trains onwards to Exeter. The 1,092yd long tunnel was the most important engineering feature on the B&E and its maximum depth below the surface was 199½ ft. Work on it began early in 1842 and over 1,000 navvies were used. Fourteen shafts were sunk to speed up the work by increasing the number of faces which could be excavated. One of the four contractors went bankrupt, but by February 1844 the tunnel was finished except for the ballasting and laying the permanent way. The works between Cullompton and Exeter, started in March 1843, were not quite complete.

Between Whiteball Tunnel and Exeter were four timber bridges over the River Culm and two across the River Exe. These lasted for 60 years until replaced by steel girders. The station at Exeter St David's was unusual to modern eyes inasmuch as both the arrival and departure platforms were on the down, or city side of the line.

The completed B&E was opened on 1 May 1844 and the cost of the whole railway did not exceed the £2m authorised by Parliament and in those days, keeping to the budget was a rare thing.

The B&E wished to save capital by not purchasing locomotives and rolling stock, so persuaded the GWR to work the line. This gave the Great Western a main line of 194 miles, which at that time was the longest in the kingdom.

On 1 May all business was suspended in Exeter. Numerous bands played and there was a feeling of great jollity. A special train from Bristol conveying the railway's directors arrived about 12.30pm, the two engines drawing it decorated with flags and banners. The first through train from London arrived shortly after. This carried the GWR directors and was driven personally by Sir Daniel Gooch, the locomotive superintendent. At 5.20pm Sir Daniel drove the return train which arrived at Paddington at 10.00pm. Sir Thomas Acland who had travelled on that train, went straight to the House of Commons and by 10.30pm stood up and told the House that he had been in Exeter at 5.20. This was a great achievement in those days. The railway had reduced a 16½ hour journey to only 4½ hours and at half the price of road travel.

The arrival of the B&E caused an extra minute hand to be added to a clock in Fore Street, Exeter, in order to show railway, as opposed to local time On 2 November 1852 the Dean of Exeter directed that the cathedral clock be advanced 14 minutes to show Greenwich, or railway time.

In 1849 the B&E's financial position allowed it to become completely independent and have its own locomotives and rolling stock. In May that year the company possessed 20 passenger and 8 goods engine and one combined locomotive and carriage. By the time the B&E was taken over by the GWR on 1 January 1876, the locomotive stock had increased to 107. Locomotive workshops had been opened at Bristol in 1854 and turned out their first completed locomotive in 1859, building some 30 others during the next 16 years. Until 1860 the engines were painted a dark green picked out with black, but subsequently the colour scheme changed to all-over black. Coaches were painted a dark crimson lake, so dark that it appeared almost black.

Apart from the main line, B&E branches ran to several towns in Somerset and in Devon to Tiverton, the total mileage being no less than 213. The main line in Devon was converted to mixed gauge 1 March 1876.

The broad gauge was safe and stable. For example, on 8 February 1855 an up express due at Tiverton Junction about 9.30pm was late due to the weather. A goods train arrived first, so signals were placed at danger to halt the express. The snow fell so thickly that the express driver failed to see the red warning lights until he was very near the station. Consequently the express struck the goods train which destroyed half of a brick building. 'Fortunately, although the shock was felt by passengers in the express train, none of them were injured beyond some slight bruises. The engine of the express train was disabled, and was unable to proceed' – *Gloucester Journal* 17 February 1855.

Stations on the B&E were relatively sparse, there being none between Wellington and Tiverton Road (it became Tiverton Junction in 1848), until Burlescombe was added in 1867. Local pressure for a station at Sampford Peverell was somewhat appeased by the provision of a single goods siding laid in 1895. In 1907 further requests for a station were rejected, but 21 years later the GWR yielded and erected a simple halt, the total cost being £2,130 including the price of lengthening the siding. This halt opened on 9 July 1928.

B&E 2-2-2WT No 33 at Tiverton Junction. The photograph could not have been taken in 1848 as the writing suggests because the engine was not built until 1851. Author's collection

Hardly was the paint dry on the platform shelters when the government announced that to assist unemployment it would fund certain railway improvements. Growing summer holiday traffic, although welcome on the financial side, was becoming an embarrassment to the running department as on summer Saturdays the two lines between Taunton and Newton Abbot were chock-a-block with trains.

A solution was to quadruple the track in certain places, one of the suggested areas being between Sampford Peverell and Tiverton Junction. In the event this was curtailed to the existing tracks remaining at Sampford Peverell as through roads, new platforms being built further back and served by loop lines, thus giving expresses an opportunity to overtake stopping passenger or goods trains.

The new layout included an additional goods siding north of the Up passenger platform. The re-organisation demanded a new signal box be built at the other end of the station, but even so, some of the points were so far from the box that they could not be worked by mechanical rodding and were required to be operated by electric motors, power being derived from a hand-cranked generator. During the changeover to four tracks, the original platforms remained in use, the new ones being built behind them. The new Up platform came into use on 7 February and the new Down platform on 6 March 1932.

As an economy measure in September 1955 the station was partly unstaffed and completely so on 3 October 1960. The end was now near. On 9 September 1963 Sampford Peverell closed to goods and then to passengers on 5 October 1964 when the local passenger service between Taunton and Exeter was withdrawn. On 10 March 1968 the former loops, by then

Tiverton Junction, view Up from the signal box 28 January 1932 before the line was quadrupled. Author's collection

converted into sidings, were taken out of use and the signal box closed. The station seemed to have gone for ever...but not so.

Until 1972 British Rail held the concept of passenger stations being in the centre of a large built-up area; then on 1 May 1972 a new idea was born. Bristol Parkway station opened on the site of a redundant marshalling yard. Although in a fairly rural situation, it proved highly convenient to motorists from Bristol, Bath and the new town of Yate, who could drive to the station and use the free car park there – much pleasanter than driving to a city centre station encountering frustrating traffic problems en route and parking difficulties on arrival. The idea caught on and Parkway stations were opened in various parts of the country. Tiverton Parkway, on the site of Sampford Peverell station, was opened officially on 5 May 1986 and to the public on 12 May, replacing Tiverton Junction which closed on 11 May. Tiverton Parkway is adjacent to the junction of the North Devon Link Road and the M5. Its buildings are in beautiful dark rust-coloured brick.

Cullompton has enjoyed various spellings and presumably in order to be fair, in 1858 the *Tiverton Gazette* printed the B&E time table with Down trains calling at Cullompton and up trains at Collompton. The B&E officially adopted the latter spelling in its December 1867 time table.

Because Exeter City Council refused to allow the B&E to construct a station, or even run a railway through any portion of the city, perforce the station had to be built at Red Cow village. To avoid the necessity of passengers and baggage having to cross the tracks, Brunel's one-sided design was used with both platforms on the same side of the line, the Up platform logically to the north, and the Down to the south. The South Devon Railway later leased accommodation and each company provided its own station master.

When the LSWR was granted running powers, this station would have been unable to cope with the additional traffic so a new station was planned. The B&E engineer Francis Fox designed the roof and Henry Lloyd the buildings. The platforms were covered by a train shed. The platform nearest the city was for GWR Down trains; the central island platform for LSWR

Cullompton, view Up before the 1931 quadrupling. Author's collection

Silverton circa 1905. Notice the observatory in the stationmaster's garden. Author's collection

The track in the Stoke Canon area was liable to flooding. A 43XX class 2-6-0 carrying the express headcode, draws what appears to be a two coach stopping train through the 1929 floods. Author's collection

View Down from Exeter West signal box, 6 August 1984. Author

Achilles class 4-2-2 No 3009 *Flying Dutchman* at the Down end of Exeter St David's circa 1900. The handle on the cab side is to shut off the water in the event of a gauge glass shattering. Author's collection

West Country class Pacific No 34009 *Lyme Regis* at Exeter St David's circa 1949. Although the view is Down, it is a Down SR express because at that station WR and SR Down trains face the opposite direction. No 34009 is in the Bulleid livery of malachite green and gold, but with a BR number. A luggage bridge can be seen above the locomotive. Author's collection

A ballast train from Meldon Quarry leaves Exeter St David's for Exeter Central 10 May 1956, headed by Ivatt class 2 2-6-2T No 41307 and N class 2-6-0 No 31842. Banking at the rear are E1R class ex-London, Brighton & South Coast Railway 0-6-2Ts No 32135 and No 32124. R.T.Coxon

A Morris
Commercial van at
Exeter, July 1931.
Although in Messrs
Cadbury's livery, it
was operated by
the GWR on
contractor hire and
bore the GWR No
2371. Author's
collection

trains in both directions and the western island platform for LSWR Down
and GWR Up trains. Baggage was raised to the luggage bridge by hydraulic
lifts. St David's became the busiest station in South West England, an honour
it still retains.

4 Broad Gauge Lines: The South Devon Railway

PARLIAMENT AUTHORISING the B&E prompted enterprising inhabitants of Plymouth to extend the railway to their town, but funds could not be raised. Exeter was unenthusiastic for J.B. Baron Collins wrote in the January 1913 *Railway Magazine*: 'Exeter people hoped that no lines would be constructed west of their city so that traffic should not pass without being much handled and passengers also, as far as their money was concerned. Bed and meals for a few hours at least, and then a coach journey to the regions beyond were thought more paying for Exeter than being what it has become, an excellent railway centre'. The idea of an extension was not forgotten by Plymouth and on 4 July 1844 the South Devon Railway bill received Royal Assent. Brunel was appointed engineer and his employment proved highly expensive. Always keen on fresh ideas, he believed that the atmospheric system patented by the brothers Jacob and Joseph Samuda to be ideal for taking trains over the severe gradients, some as steep as 1 in 36 – very steep for a main line railway.

The former atmospheric railway pumping house at Exeter St David's. Author's collection

With the atmospheric system, locomotives were dispensed with and replaced by a special carriage with a piston slung beneath fitting into a pipe from which air was pumped out by stationary engines placed beside the track every two to three miles. The pipe necessarily had a slot in its top through which the strut linking the piston to the carriage, could pass. This slot was sealed by a leather strip. George and Robert Stephenson scoffed at the atmospheric railway as being 'a rope of wind'.

The SDR was built as a single line and was safer than other single lines as due to the system of working, two trains colliding head-on was impossible. The 15 miles between Exeter St David's and Teignmouth were opened to passenger traffic on 30 May 1846 with locomotives hired from the GWR. Early in 1847 experimental atmospheric trains were run. Locomotives worked goods trains from 1 May 1847 and the line was extended to Totnes 20 July 1847, goods traffic starting 6 December 1847. On 13 September 1847 atmospheric working was used for passenger trains Exeter to Teignmouth and the highest speed reached was 68mph hauling a train of 28 tons. Atmospheric working was extended to Newton Abbot on 10 January 1848.

Problems were looming. Lack of telegraphic communication meant that the engine houses did not know when a train was approaching and so consumed coal when it was unnecessary to create a vacuum. Frosts prevented the valve from closing properly. Other problems were that the leather flap deteriorated, partly through the vacuum sucking out natural oils and the salt-laden air beside the sea made matters worse. Another disadvantage was that because the pipe could not run through points, starting a train from a loop towards a single line was a problem. It was overcome by using an auxiliary pipe containing a piston with a rope attached which could be coupled to the train. When the piston carriage reached the main pipe, the rope was released. The pumping engines were unreliable and broke down. These problems resulted in atmospheric traction being suspended 10 September 1848 and it was never revived. It had cost approximately £427,000 of which only about £50,000 was recouped from the sale of redundant plant.

There were those who saw with regret the end of the atmospheric railway. The Rev. Treasurer Hawker wrote in 1885: 'I remember travelling by the atmospheric from Newton to Exeter. The motion was very smooth and pleasant; no screaming whistle but a melodious horn was sounded on nearing the stations reminding one of the coaching days of old; no puffing or labouring up the inclines but a swift silent even progress unhasting, unresting; no coke dust or sulphurous smell from the engine'.

Meanwhile on 5 May 1848 the line was extended from Totnes to Laira Green, east of Plymouth, and to Plymouth Millbay on 2 April 1849. Some of the viaducts were graceful timber spans on masonry piers. Gradients were very severe. Dainton Bank between Newton Abbot and Totnes consisted of five miles ascent and descent with gradients as steep as 1 in 36, and Rattery Bank 20 miles between Totnes and Plymouth included about 1½ miles of 1 in 42 – extremely testing for the early locomotives. The SDR was worked by the GWR.

Initially the sea wall in the Dawlish area gave no trouble, the problem being caused by rain when a cliff slipped on 29 December 1852. The sea was responsible for trouble in 1855 and has continued to be so since. Faced with

West Country class Pacific No 34001 *Exeter* in malachite green and with an unlettered tender, at Dawlish with the 5.45pm Down stopping train from St David's, 2 July 1949. It was a regular SR turn to keep Southern crews familiar with the WR route. John Bamsey

Nine camping coaches at Dawlish, August 1968. Alan Dorrington

Storm damage by Parson's Tunnel, west of Dawlish, 16 February 1855. Passengers from both trains use a temporary diversionary footpath. Author's collection

Up broad gauge express hauled by a Rover class 4-2-2 on the sea wall at Teignmouth 6 July 1884. Author's collection

View Down at Teignmouth 18 March 1894, slewing the up line. Men are standing on the widened platform. The train sheds have been removed, but their marks can be seen on the side of the footbridge which has been given temporary supports. Author's collection

steep charges for maintenance and the renewal of the permanent way, the SDR amalgamated with the GWR on 1 February 1876.

The SDR was continued on to Penzance by the Cornwall Railway whose Act was passed 3 August 1846. The Royal Albert Bridge across the River Tamar was the principal engineering feature and to comply with Admiralty requirements it needed two spans of 465ft and a clear headway of 100ft. Work began in July 1853 on the central pier. The arched truss for the main spans were erected on the Devonshire bank, floated into position and raised by hydraulic jacks. Brunel's chief assistant, R.P. Brereton was really responsible for the bridge which opened 4 May 1859. Cornishmen claim that this bridge 'ties England to Cornwall'.

It is not always realised that railways had to compete with coastal steamers. A London to Plymouth third class railway ticket cost 18s 8d in the eighteen-eighties, whereas Irish steamers calling there charged only 7s 0d for deck passengers, or 15s 0d should a cabin be required.

The last down broad gauge train, the 5.00pm Paddington to Plymouth, ran over the SDR on 20 May 1892. The Night Mail at 9.00pm was standard gauge for the first time and used mixed gauge track to Exeter and then travelled over the LSWR route to Plymouth as it did on the two subsequent nights. The very last broad gauge train was the 9.45pm Up from Penzance and the Chief Inspector travelling on it was required to ascertain from each stationmaster that all broad gauge stock had been despatched. Conversion work began on 21 May and standard gauge traffic commenced on Monday 23 May.

Men had been brought to the area by special train from other parts of the GWR and set down at various bases. Where possible they were accommodated in station offices and goods sheds, otherwise 63 bed-space tents were provided plus a straw-filled bag and two rugs for each man.

In October 1904 a Great Central Railway locomotive accomplished one of the longest runs in the country – an excursion from Manchester, London Road, to Plymouth and return. It left Manchester at 11.30pm on 28 October and reached Plymouth at 9.50am the following morning, 15 minutes early, having covered the 374 miles in 10 hours 20 minutes including stops. It had a load of five GCR bogie coaches to Exeter where two GWR bogies were added. It left Plymouth 10 minutes late at 12.03am on 30 October and arrived Manchester 9.50am.

WW1 did not have too much impact on the line, though staff shortages caused problems and Exeter St Thomas station closed 2 April 1917. It was probably the most important station on the GWR which suffered this indignity and was not re-opened until 3 March 1919.

WW2 saw GWR locomotives and crews working SR trains between Exeter and Plymouth and likewise SR locomotives and crews working GWR trains between these places in order to give them the necessary route knowledge in the event of a line being blocked by enemy action. An armoured train based at Newton Abbot patrolled between Kingswear and Exeter primarily as defence against sea or seaplane attack. On 20 August 1940 nine bombs dropped on Newton Abbot station killing 14 persons and severely damaging five locomotives. The railway was closed for 10 hours while an unexploded bomb was removed. In 1941 Plymouth North Road station was bombed, two people killed and Millbay station damaged. The locomotive shed was completely destroyed. On 3 May 1941 St David's station, locomotive shed, goods shed and signal boxes were bombed. The air raid shelter in the station yard received a direct hit and eight men sheltering there were killed.

From 1945 holidays with pay meant that many visitors arrived by train, usually on a Saturday. Many of the trains returning passengers to their homes required regulation tickets to be obtained. These were free, printed with the train letter and number and the holder only permitted to travel on that train. When all regulation tickets for a certain train were issued, passengers were offered a seat on an alternative service. A regulation ticket entitled the holder to a place on the train, not a particular seat.

The first diesel-hydraulic locomotives arrived in 1958, the South West having been selected for early dieselisation owing to the distance coal had to be hauled from the pits and having gradients which could be more easily tackled by diesel engines. 1961 was the last summer when steam locomotives were used in any numbers

When opened on 30 May 1846 Exeter St Thomas comprised a single platform sheltered by a train shed. As it was the SDR's headquarters, an imposing frontage contained the company's offices. Nine-tenths of the SDR's traffic for Exeter used St Thomas, as it was both nearer the commercial centre

Exeter St Thomas, view Up. The Down platform is longer than the Up. Author's collection

and the distance travelled by rail less, saving both time and money. Glass was removed from the train shed in the nineteen-fifties and the remaining skeleton removed in 1971.

The original station at Newton Abbot was of the single-sided pattern similar to that at St David's with Up and Down platforms and train sheds both on the west side of the line. A third shed was provided for Torquay branch trains. Between 1859 and 1861 these sheds were demolished and the station rebuilt to the conventional pattern. It was further reconstructed 1925 to 1927 being formally reopened with two island platforms 11 April 1927. Adjoining were wagon works and a locomotive factory.

Plymouth North Road was designed by P.J. Margery, the SDR's engineer, for use by his company and also the LSWR. The station buildings were joint

43XX class 2-6-0 No 6385 at Newton Abbot 13 July 1956. This engine was one of the first of its class to wear the BR lined green livery. On 8 May 1956 No 6385 and No 6372 worked the Royal Train from Taunton to Barnstaple. For this duty, instead of the unlined black as hitherto carried, they were painted green and fully lined out and the safety valve covers polished. That autumn it became official policy to repaint the whole class unlined green and in February 1957, full lining was added. Newton Abbot wagon works can be seen in the background. Colin Roberts

At Dainton Warship class diesel-hydraulic D801 *Vanguard* works the 6.25am Penzance to Paddington, while 4-6-0 No 5967 *Bickmarsh Hall*, now preserved, and No 4075 *Cardiff Castle* head a train to Plymouth, 16 May 1959. Michael Jenkins

4-6-0 No 6833 *Calcot Grange* pauses at Dainton Summit with a Down freight train 12 August 1955. The sidings on each side of the main line are level. R.E.Toop

4-6-0 No 6008 *King James II* climbs to Dainton with the 'Cornish Riviera Express' 12 August 1955. Steam is being emitted from an unauthorised place. R.E.Toop

Trains cross on Dainton Bank: the Up 'Cornishman' is headed by Castle class 4-6-0 No 7000 *Viscount Portal* and No 6940 *Didlington Hall*, while No 5920 *Wycliffe Hall* heads a Newton Abbot to Plymouth train 12 August 1955. R.E.Toop

The train sheds at Totnes, view Up. The signal box, right, opened in 1894, closed 7 January 1923. Notice the forward extension to improve the signalman's sighting. Author's collection

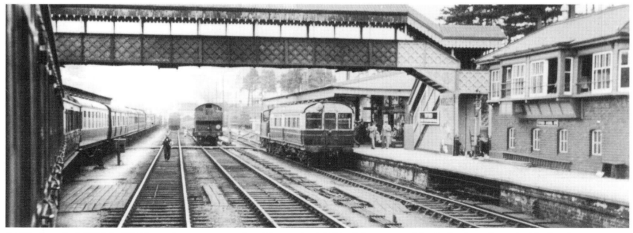

3150 class 2-6-2T No 3166 on the centre road at Totnes in 1947 with a target No 3 displayed, probably having returned after banking. 48XX class 0-4-2T No 4867 is ready to propel the auto coach to Ashburton. E.J.M. Hayward

5101 class 2-6-2T No 4165 and No 5174 waiting at Totnes to pilot and bank up Rattery Incline, the freight train seen in the next image, 12 August 1960. R.E.Toop

2-6-2T No 4165 and 4-6-0 No 4991 *Cobham Hall*, with 2-6-2T No 5174 as banker, wait at Totnes for a clear signal, 12 August 1960. R.E.Toop

Totnes station garden in 1926 when it won the GWR 'Best Kept Station' cup. Author's collection

Railway wagons at Totnes Quay in the 1920s. L.F. Folkard collection

The Great Western Society's preserved 4-6-0 No 6998 *Burton Agnes Hall* and 1361 class 0-6-0ST No 1363 at Totnes Quay, May 1966. R.A. Lumber

4575 class 2-6-2T No 5558 at Brent running round the branch train 17 August 1955. Probably most of the passengers it carried from Kingsbridge are waiting on the Up platform. The goods yard is quiet. R.E.Toop

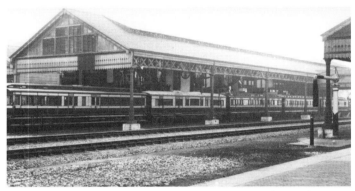

The Royal Train on the Up track at Plymouth North Road station 10 March 1902, hauled by Bulldog class 4-4-0 No 3357 *Royal Sovereign*. Formerly named *Exeter*, it was temporarily renamed for working this special. In October 1903 it was renamed *Smeaton* to avoid confusion with No 3442 *City of Exeter*. In broad gauge days, the water crane on the right may have been able to serve a locomotive on either track. Author's collection

Snow plough No B965238 and No B965239 at Plymouth Laira shed 6 April 1993. Author

64XX class 0-6-0PT No 6414 at Plymouth North Road with a motor train to Saltash 7 July 1958. R.A.Lumber

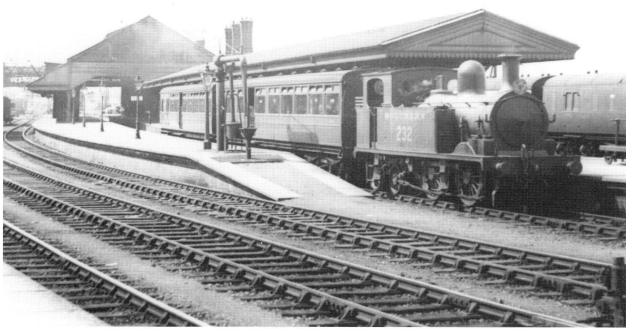

Circa 1936 SR 02 class 0-4-4T No 232 leaves Plymouth North Road with a train of gated stock for Friary station. Lens of Sutton

Transferring mail from *Sir Walter Raleigh* to the railway at Plymouth Docks. In 2 ½ hours of working, a conveyor carried 52 tons. Author's collection

property, but the tracks belonged solely to the SDR. The station consisted of two train sheds covering the main platforms, with two through roads between the sheds. Construction was of timber due to the fact that the line was on an embankment and any heavier material may have caused the station to subside. As at St David's, there was the curious situation of trains from Waterloo leaving in the opposite direction to those for Paddington. Plymouth North Road was enlarged in 1908 and further developed in 1939. By 1956 the old timber buildings were life-expired and the station was rebuilt, the new station opened by Dr Richard Beeching 26 March 1962. A new power signal box, one of the first on the WR, opened 26 November 1960. From 1904 steam rail motors – a combined coach and locomotive – worked local services, but from

1914 were replaced by 0-6-0PTs and auto coaches, the locomotives often sandwiched between two coaches at each end.

A new four road terminus was opened at Millbay in 1900 but closed 23 April 1941. In the vicinity were carriage sheds. Millbay Docks were important in the days of passenger liners as GWR tenders collected passengers and mail from them and for those in a hurry, this was quicker than going on to Southampton. Ocean mail trains were fast and on 9 May 1904 *City of Truro* reached the record speed of 102.3mph. In 1906 the first non-stop run was made between Plymouth and Paddington. During 1948 355,365 ocean mail bags and 5,760 passengers were handled at Millbay Docks from 119 liners. 61 special trains were provided for ocean passengers in 1951 in addition to 39 mail trains.

The exterior of the timber-built Torre station circa 1965. Lens of Sutton

The SDR Act of 28 August 1846 permitted a line to be constructed from Aller Junction, west of Newton Abbot, to Torre. This single track, broad gauge line opened on 18 December 1848 and was continued to Kingswear by the Dartmouth & Torbay Railway Act which received Royal Assent 27 July 1857. A leading light of this latter company was Charles Seale Hayne who operated river steamers to feed the SDR at Totnes and also founded the nearby agricultural college. The line opened to Paignton on 2 August 1859. The opening was certainly memorable as it was celebrated with a large baked pudding made in eight portions. When joined together it weighed 1½ tons. It contained 573lb of flour; 382lb of raisins; 191lb of currants; 191lb of bread; 382lb of suet; a 'great number of eggs'; 360 quarts of milk; 320 lemons; 95lb of sugar and 144 nutmegs. It cost £45 and the pudding was drawn by eight horses to Paignton Green where the public dinner took place.

On 27 May 1930 Fordson tractors haul horse floats to the Bath & West Agricultural Show held at Torre. Author's collection

4-6-0 No 4906 *Bradfield Hall* leaves Torquay with a Down train circa 1930. Author's collection

For passengers the line was extended to Brixham Road (later renamed Churston) 14 March 1861 and to freight 1 April 1861. Passenger traffic opened to the terminus at Kingswear 16 August 1864 and to goods 2 April 1866. The SDR worked the line and absorbed it 1 January 1872. It was believed that Kingswear would be served by some transatlantic liners and a large hotel was built, but these hopes were never fulfilled. The line was converted to standard gauge 20 to 23 May 1892.

4-6-0 No 4985 *Allesley Hall* leaves the coaching stock yard at Goodrington 9 August 1962. Mile post showing 222 ¾ from Paddington is between the photographer and the signal box. R.E.Toop

4-6-0 No 5994 *Roydon Hall* approaches Churston with an Exeter to Kingswear train, 17 August 1961. Line 'monuments' for correcting the track alignment can be seen in the ballast to the right of the train. R.E.Toop

4-6-0 No 5028
Llantilio Castle
approaches
Churston with the
Down 'Torbay
Express' 13 August
1955. 14XX class
0-4-2T No 1427 is
in charge of the
Brixham 'Whippet'.
R.E.Toop

BR closed the line south of Paignton 31 October 1972, the Dart Valley Railway taking it over as the Torbay Steam Railway. The preserved railway opened a new station at Paignton on the site of BR's down carriage sidings. When the Buckfast line became independent, the Torbay Steam Railway changed its name to the Paignton & Dartmouth Steam Railway.

Torre station is a Grade II listed building of Italianate design and originally named Torquay and formed the terminus until the extension to Paignton opened 2 August 1859. Until closure to goods 4 December 1967, it remained the freight railhead as no goods facilities were provided at Torquay station.

The present Torquay station, in French pavilion style with a cast iron crest to its roof, opened in 1873 to replace the first building. Both platforms have an

Poster announcing
reduced fare,
17.7.1933 for the
Kingswear –
Dartmouth ferry.

Tickets: Sea Mills –
Paignton; Seat
Regulation Tickets;
3-part
rail/steamer/rail;
Kingswear platform
ticket

4575 class 2-6-2T No 4582 on 27 July 1953 ascends the bank near Churston with coal which had arrived at Kingswear by sea for Torquay gas works. Beyond the brake van can be seen a board warning Down goods trains to stop and apply wagon brakes. R.E.Toop

DMU set P200 calls at Britannia Halt in June 1972, the last year of BR working the line. R.E.Toop

4-6-0 No 7004 *Eastnor Castle* approaches Kingswear with the Down 'Torbay Express' 8 August 1955. R.E.Toop

BR Standard class 9 2-10-0 No 92136 from Newport shed, leaves Kingswear 30 July 1960 with the 5.30pm to Exeter carrying a through coach to Taunton. This class of engine was normally used on heavy freight workings. R.E.Toop

4-6-0 No 4920 *Dumbleton Hall,* now preserved, arrives at Kingswear with a stopping train 8 August 1955. On the left is 4-6-0 No 7004 *Eastnor Castle* which had arrived with the 'Torbay Express'. A corridor connection door leans against the signal box. R.E.Toop

attractive arcade with decorative canopy supports imaginatively painted to reveal their features. The station was a hive of activity on summer Saturdays and seat regulation had to be enforced.

Between Goodrington and Kingswear the line is very scenic. Approaching Kingswear the railway originally crossed Longwood and Noss Creeks by timber viaducts, but on 20 May 1923 the line was re-routed around these inlets. The quayside sidings at Kingswear were principally for the transfer of coal arriving by sea for general use and Torquay gas works, this traffic ending in the nineteen-fifties. When a vessel discharged, about six trainloads were sent up the branch. Dartmouth station was on a pontoon and although it had no railway trains, due to the Royal Naval College traffic, the station master was of a higher grade than his colleague at Kingswear! *The Mew* was the well-loved ferry steamer owned by the GWR which worked from Kingswear to Dartmouth from 20 May 1908 until 8 October 1954. Although sent to Dover at the time of the Dunkirk evacuation, *The Mew* was not used as its draught was too great to get to the beach and she was too small to carry large numbers from offshore. The Kingswear line was served by several named trains including the Torbay Express, the Devonian and the Torquay Pullman, which was short-lived, there being little demand for a luxury service at a higher price. Coaches from the Cornish Riviera Express were slipped at Exeter St David's.

View of the trackless Dartmouth station from the road. Author's collection

5 Branches from the Great Western Railway Main Line

The Devon & Somerset Railway

The broad gauge Devon & Somerset Railway (DSR) which received its Act on 29 July 1864 to construct a line between Norton Fitzwarren and Barnstaple, was beset by many vicissitudes. The Somerset portion was delayed through lack of finance and navvies catching cholera and the Devon section to Barnstaple was not opened until 1 November 1873.

The DSR made an expensive mistake. When the line was being built, Richard Hassard, its engineer, had a conversation with Henry Ellis, a director of the B&E which held the contract to work the line. Ellis remarked that if the DSR approached his fellow directors they would probably approve of standard gauge being laid. This suggestion was ignored and broad gauge laid, thus costing thousands of pounds more for construction, and also for ultimate conversion.

On 1 August 1876 the B&E was amalgamated with the GWR which took over the working agreement. The last broad gauge train ran over the DSR on 14 May 1881 and a standard gauge goods and two passenger trains were operated on 18 May, a full service being run the following day. The DSR was sold to the GWR on 1 July 1901. One interesting train on the line was the daily rabbit special from South Molton, but myxomatosis ended that traffic. With the development of road transport, the line became uneconomic, losing £80,000 annually and the last train ran on 1 October 1966.

The DSR entered Devon at Venn Cross 666ft above sea level. Although most of the station was in Somerset, the west

Excess fare ticket Morebath to Taunton, 27 August 1966.

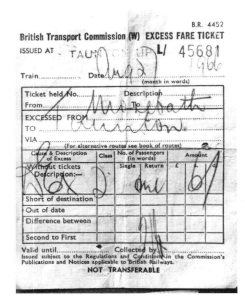

BR Standard class 3 2-6-2T No 82001 works the 16.20 Taunton to Barnstaple 30 May 1964. The passing loop at Morebath has been lifted and the signal box is in the course of demolition.
R.A.Lumber

The fireman of the tank engine hauling the Taunton to Barnstaple train takes the single line tablet from the Morebath Junction signalman. 43XX class 2-6-0 No 7337 (83B Taunton) waits with an Up stopping train.
T.J.Saunders

A Down train is waved away from Morebath Junction Halt by the guard.
T.J.Saunders

end of the platform and the goods shed were in Devon. Beyond Venn Cross the line descended to Morebath Junction where the Exe Valley branch joined (see page 60). Morebath Junction Halt opened 1 December 1928 and was interesting in as much that its approach could be muddy, so Wellington boots were often worn to the station where passengers changed into shoes, leaving their boots below the waiting shelter seat. The next station, Dulverton was in Somerset. Just before East Anstey, 700ft above sea level, the line returned to Devon. Half a mile beyond South Molton was an exchange siding with the Florence Mining Company's tramway, the ironstone being carried by rail to Bridgwater. South Molton was a busy station and dealt with 600 to 700 wagons monthly. Filleigh station, known as Castle Hill until 1 January 1881, was used by pupils and staff of West Buckland School. The GWR lorry delivered from Filleigh to Parracombe and Lynton, avoiding consignees having to collect items. The Lynton & Barnstaple Railway had no lorry delivery service and this was one of the reasons for its closure.

As a link at Barnstaple with the LSWR's Exeter to Ilfracombe line was desirable, an Act of 31 July 1885 authorised a connecting spur which opened on 1 June 1887 and permitted the GWR to operate through trains to Ilfracombe. From about 1925 the 43XX class 2-6-0s handled most of this traffic and in order not to foul structures on the Ilfracombe line which had a more restrictive loading gauge, their steps had to be cut back to a width of

Tickets: Barnstaple Junction, Ilfracombe, Yelverton, Princetown, King Tor, Okehampton, Dousland, Morebath, Sampford Courtenay, Plymouth.

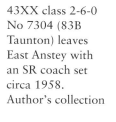

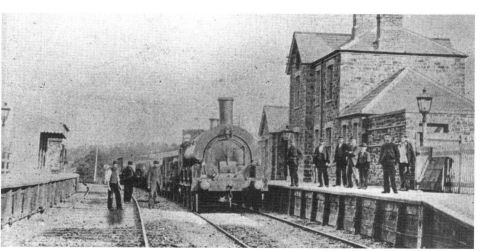

Luggage labels: Molland, Tavistock, Barnstaple, Morebath.

43XX class 2-6-0 No 7304 (83B Taunton) leaves East Anstey with an SR coach set circa 1958. Author's collection

43XX class 2-6-0 No 5344 passes Bishop's Nympton & Molland with a Down five coach Saturday express, 21 June 1958. R.J.Sellick

A 0-6-0ST heads a Down broad gauge goods at South Molton in 1874. The track has cross sleepers rather than the longitudinal type more commonly found on this gauge. Author's collection

View of Filleigh
Viaduct from the
rear of a Taunton
to Barnstaple train.
T.J.Saunders

An oil lamp at
Filleigh station
circa 1936.
Author's collection

At Swimbridge 43XX class 2-6-0 No 7333 working the 1.03pm Taunton to Barnstaple Junction, crosses sister engine No 6372 working the 2.24pm Barnstaple Junction to Taunton 11 May 1963. No 6372 was one of the engines which hauled the Royal Train over the line on 8 May 1956. R.E.Toop

The timber-built Barnstaple Victoria Road station is centre left; a gas tank wagon for recharging coach lighting and restaurant cars, centre, and a cattle wagon on the far right. The locomotive is probably an Armstrong 0-6-0. Author's collection

43XX class 2-6-0 No 4304 at Barnstaple circa 1930. An ROP (Russian Oil Products) petrol tanker is the third vehicle in the train, while a BP petrol lorry is on the right. For safety, the two shunters carry their poles vertically. R.T.Clements collection

A train staff ticket which a driver would be given for authority to proceed if the actual train staff needed retention for a following train.

8ft 4in. A two road engine shed constucted of timber was provided at Barnstaple, Victoria Road. It closed in January 1951 after which WR engines used the former Southern Railway shed at Barnstaple Junction. The DSR passenger terminus at Victoria Road was constructed of timber. It closed to passenger traffic 13 June 1960. Following the closure of the line to Norton Fitzwarren, Victoria Road remained open for goods traffic until 5 March 1970.

The Culm Valley Light Railway

The Culm Valley Light Railway (CVLR) Act was passed on 15 May 1873 to construct a line from Tiverton Junction to Hemyock. Its engineer was Arthur Pain, trained by R.P. Brereton, Brunel's chief assistant. Pain had the then novel idea of how to construct a relatively cheap line in an area where an ordinary railway would not be an economic proposition. His proposal was encouraged by the Regulation of Railways Act passed in 1868 where a 'light railway' could be constructed, allowing a maximum weight of eight tons per axle and a speed limit of 25mph. Stations and signalling were allowed to be simpler. Pain anticipated costs of £3,000 per mile rather than the £15,000 of the Seaton branch line.

Unfortunately the contractor's work was unsatisfactory and some work had to be redone. The line eventually opened on 29 May 1876, but its accounts were far from healthy: expenditure was £42,902 and receipts only £24,121. In July 1876 H. Cecil Newton was appointed secretary of the CVLR, he already held similar posts in the Torbay & Brixham Railway and the Buckfastleigh, Totnes & South Devon Railway – so he had experienced problems of small railways having to deal with a larger company – the CVLR was worked by the GWR.

14XX class 0-4-2T No 1440 leaves Tiverton Junction 12 October 1957 with the 1.40pm to Hemyock. R.E.Toop

48XX class 0-4-2T No 4827 at Uffculme en route to Tiverton Junction circa 1946. The locomotive's number is painted on the buffer beam as was GWR standard practice. Author's collection

View of the level crossing gates at Culmstock from the veranda of a goods brake van 31 August 1965. The cap of the sand hopper is seen centre bottom, and the brake handle to the right. Michael Farr

14XX class 0-4-2T No 1421 calls at Whitehall Halt with the 2.45pm from Hemyock 8 June 1963. Author

Empty milk tankers being hauled over the road at Hemyock into the factory, 28 October 1975. A man holds a 'Stop' board. Col M.H.Cobb

The GWR could have been more helpful. There was a race course at Uffculme, but the *Tiverton Gazette* of 5 September 1876 reported: 'The GWR did not offer travelling facilities to intending visitors. For instance, a reduced fare of one penny with the disadvantage of having to wait several hours before the sports actually commenced, was simply a mockery of the public. Excursionists were few and most travelled by ordinary trains.'

Instead of the projected income of £10 per mile per week, the reality proved to be an income of just over £4. The CVLR had almost no money available to cover the overdraft and certainly none available for the ordinary shareholders who had been promised five per cent. The line was sold to the GWR on 5 August 1880.

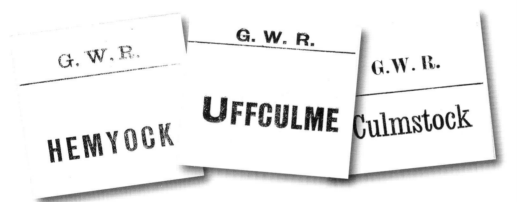

In 1885 three Hemyock farmers, John Clist, Samuel Farrant and Edward Lutley discussed means of countering the agricultural depression. A recent development was the centrifugal milk separator which was eminently suited to large scale production. In 1886 the Culm Valley Dairy Company was formed, the first mechanical butter factory in the West of England. Butter was despatched by rail. The by-product was skimmed milk which was fed to pigs and pigs provided more rail traffic, while an animal feed mill at Culmstock provided yet further traffic. In 1916 the Wilts United Dairies acquired the Culm Valley Dairy, ceased making butter and concentrated on liquid milk for the London market. In May 1927 United Dairies operated the first rail bulk milk tanks to run in England and from 1932 used them to carry milk from Hemyock. Other regular traffic on the line was worsted cloth from Coldharbour Mill.

(Left) At Hemyock is ex-SDR converted former broad gauge 2-4-0T *Mercury*, later GWR No 1300. On the signal box is an 'S' plate, white on a red ground, indicating that the signalling is in order. (A fault was shown by a red letter on a white ground). Author's collection

(Right) 14XX class 0-4-2T No 1449 arriving at Hemyock with the 5.00pm Saturdays-only from Tiverton Junction 28 June 1958. R.E.Toop

Luggage labels: Hemyock; Uffculme; Culmstock.

14XX class 0-4-2T No 1449 leaves Hemyock 28 June 1958, with the 5.55pm to Tiverton Junction. Four milk tankers are 'inside the engine'. R.E.Toop

As the parish church at Willand was almost a mile distant, the GWR directors sanctioned the holding of two religious services a month in the waiting room at Tiverton Junction. The branch closed to passengers 9 September 1963 and to goods, excluding milk traffic, 6 September 1965. Unigate, successors to United Dairies, announced it was closing its Hemyock factory on 31 October 1975 and so the last train ran on this date, the line having missed its centenary by seven months.

Due to severe curves, only short and low height coaches could be used on the line. When the branch coaches needed replacement in 1950, the only ones found suitable were two ex-Barry Railway vehicles. Originally electrically lit, they were converted to gas lighting because speed on the CVLR was insufficient for the axle-driven dynamos to keep the batteries charged. They were the very last gas lit coaches on British Railways.

Tiverton Junction to Tiverton

An Act for this B&E branch was passed on 31 July 1845. Work was started but then delayed due to a dispute with the Grand Western Canal Company whose waterway the line had to burrow beneath at Halberton. The B&E was forced to pay £1,200 to the canal company as compensation when it was closed temporarily for the aqueduct to be built. The canal was carried at a height of 40ft in a cast iron channel supported on cast iron arches, the whole being encased in brickwork and the spaces puddled with clay to prevent leakage. Nevertheless, in cold weather it behoved the crew of the first train

14XX class 0-4-2T No 1469 at Tiverton Junction with the 12.50pm to Tiverton, 12 October 1957. R.E.Toop

14XX class 0-4-2T No 1450 arriving at Tiverton Junction with the 1.20pm ex-Tiverton 8 June 1963. No 1450 is now preserved. Author

14XX class 0-4-2T No 1450 approaching Tiverton propelling the 12.42pm ex-Tiverton Junction 8 June 1963. Author

of the day when passing under the aqueduct, to keep inside the cab to avoid being struck by an icicle.

The broad gauge branch was opened on 12 June 1848 and to prevent competition between railway and canal resulting in loss to both companies, it was agreed that the canal should carry lime, and that coal traffic should travel by rail to Taunton and then to its destination by canal. This agreement was abandoned in 1852 and coal carrying rates were so reduced that at one period the canal carried it free! Although the B&E lost an estimated £6,000, unlike the canal company it was able to recoup it elsewhere.

14XX class 0-4-2T No1440 (left) at Tiverton, while a sister engine seems to be shunting the brake van which is ex-LMS and the van ex-LNER. Author's collection

The branch was converted to standard gauge 29 June 1884 in order to form a junction with the standard gauge Tiverton & North Devon Railway which was to open on 1 August 1884. On 5 December 1927 in an effort to combat bus competition, the GWR opened a halt at Halberton. As it was situated immediately below an over bridge, cyclists, in order not to get wet saddles, left their machines under the shelter of the bridge.

Land had been bought for double track, but only single was ever laid. For over a mile each side of Halberton Halt, occupying the site of the second track, was a single row of Bramley apple trees. This curious orchard one tree wide and two miles in length was let by the GWR.

The branch could boast that it was the first in the country to have a steam railcar. Named *Fairfield*, built in 1848, it was a combined coach and locomotive. Latterly trains on the branch were worked on the push-pull system whereby an engine pulled the train in one direction and on returning pushed it, the driver controlling the engine from a special compartment at what had been the rear of the train. Passenger services were withdrawn on 5 October 1964 and freight 5 June 1967.

Stoke Canon to Morebath Junction

The railway journey from Tiverton to Exeter required a change at Tiverton Junction and a direct line was needed. The Exe Valley Railway received its Act on 30 June 1874. The line opened 1 May 1885. An extension from Tiverton to the Taunton to Barnstaple line was called for, its promoters receiving the Tiverton & North Devon Railway Act 19 July 1875. It opened 1 August 1884, some ten months before the GWR's Exe Valley branch. Although worked by the GWR, the Tiverton & North Devon retained its independence until 1 July 1894. The line from Stoke Canon to Morebath Junction eventually became uneconomic with an income of only £3,500 a year against movement costs of £21,600, so passenger and goods services were withdrawn 7 October 1963. At times it was busy and even in 1963, on Bank Holidays it was standing room only on the trains.

Tiverton was an important station, still employing a staff of 38 in 1950. In 1959 52,592 tickets were issued plus 1,055 seasons; 13,174 parcels despatched and approximately 88,000 tons of freight handled.

57XX class 0-6-0PT No 3677 at Tiverton with the 1.05pm Saturdays-only Dulverton to Exeter St David's, 28 June 1958. R.E.Toop

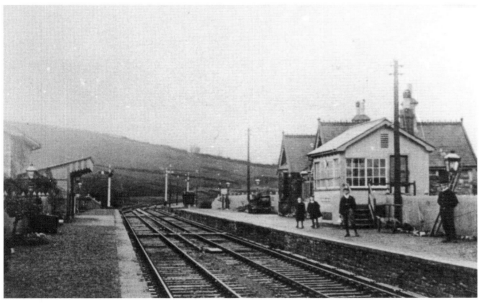

Thorverton view north circa 1910. Author's collection

Until June 1911 name boards proclaimed 'Bampton' but that month they were amended to 'Bampton (Devon)' to avoid confusion with the station of the same name on the Oxford to Witney line. When Bampton Pony Fair was held, the animals were despatched in 40 to 50 cattle wagons, but this traffic was lost to road about 1947.

Bampton view south circa 1910. A 0-6-0ST shunts near the goods shed. Author's collection

Lower Lodfin Crossing signal box was manned by Signalwoman Town for 23 years, spanning the end of the nineteenth century and the start of the twentieth, at a time when it was most unusual for a female to carry out such a duty. Although the line joined the Taunton to Barnstaple branch at Morebath Junction Halt, Exe Valley trains ran along it to terminate at Dulverton.

When floods at Brampford Speke occasionally flooded the station approach, in order to retain dry feet, passengers were dropped at Fortescue Crossing.

Exeter to Heathfield

Although the Exeter to Heathfield line latterly appeared to be a single branch, it actually comprised two railways. The first part, which received powers in the Teign Valley Railway Act 13 July 1863, allowed a line from Heathfield, on the Moretonhampstead branch, through Chudleigh to Christow. Due to various problems, mainly financial, the line was not opened until 9 October 1882 and then only to Ashton. As the Moretonhampstead branch was still broad gauge at that date, the Teign Valley line was an isolated standard gauge length.

The Exeter, Teign Valley & Chagford Railway Act of 20 August 1883 authorised a line from Exeter to Christow where it was to link with the Teign Valley Railway. This new company also experienced financial problems, caused to a large extent through measures to placate landowners. These included making two tunnels totalling 1,084yd and many cuttings. Exeter to

Ashton was not opened until 1 July 1903. Both lines were worked as one by the GWR and absorbed by that company 1 July 1923. In the GWR era, the route formed a useful by-pass to the Dawlish main line should that be blocked by storm or landslide, but following Nationalisation, the former Southern Railway's main line route to Plymouth via Okehampton was a better alternative.

The branch served important commercial premises. At Exeter, by Alphington Road Goods Junction a line trailed into the branch from the five road goods depot, two additional lines serving the Exeter Corporation Cattle market. Each Friday 500 to 600 head of cattle were loaded and up to 100 every Monday.

57XX class
0-6-0PT No 3629
shunting at Exeter
City Basin 1
October 1958.
R.A.Lumber

At Exeter Basin Loop Junction a spur opened 2 May 1904 joined the City Basin line, while in March 1958 a trailing branch from the Teign Valley line served the Marsh Barton Trading Estate including Messrs Cadbury/Fry and E. Pearce & Company. From Alphington Halt, opened 2 April 1928, the line climbed for four miles at 1 in 56 to a summit at Longdown. During WW2 a 1,100ft loop was installed here, vital for crossing diverted main line trains. It was also useful when ambulance trains headed by a London & North Eastern Railway B12 4-6-0 worked over the branch to Heathfield and thence to Moretonhampstead where the GWR's Manor House Hotel had been transformed into an army hospital.

Beyond Longdown the line descended for three miles at 1 in 64. Christow had quarry sidings. It was while constructing the line that the contractor J.H. Dickson discovered basalt and formed the Devon Basalt & Granite Company. The siding closed about 1932. To the south of Christow, Ryecroft Quarry Siding trailed in. Near Trusham were Whetcombe Quarry Siding in use 1909 until 1952 and Crockham Sidings serving the Teign Valley Granite Company. Chudleigh was interesting. Because it was set close to the River Teign and

A 0-4-2T at Ide heads a train to Heathfield. Buffer stops can be seen on the left for the end loading dock of which the track is lifted. Author's collection

517 class No 552 at Christow with the 9.45am Exeter to Heathfield circa 1905. The centre coach has a clerestory roof. Author's collection

A 517 class 0-4-2T at Trusham 1905. Having four coaches indicates that it was probably Friday, the market day, when the three-coach set required strengthening. The diamond-shaped 'T' board to the right of the station door, indicates that all is well with the telegraph. Author's collection

Chudleigh, view towards Heathfield 11 June 1921. Tree trunks are stored in the yard. Lens of Sutton

liable to flooding, a raised gangway led from the lane to a special platform for use on such occasions. South of Chudleigh Knighton Halt, opened 9 June 1924, were Ministry of Food sidings opened 22 August 1943 and lifted about 1952.

In 1934 camping coaches were brought to Ashton, followed in later years by vehicles at Chudleigh and Ide. Branch passenger services were withdrawn on 9 June 1958 and goods services gradually curtailed, final closure being on 4 December 1967.

Churston to Brixham

On 25 July 1864 Royal Assent was granted to the Torbay & Brixham Railway Act permitting a two mile long branch to be built from Churston to Brixham. A very unusual feature of this railway company was that it was practically entirely owned by just one man, R.W. Wolston. He held £17,700 of the £18,000 capital, the remaining £300 taken up by two of his relatives and a friend.

The single track, broad gauge line opened to passengers on 28 February 1868 and to freight 1 May that same year. Wolston purchased *Queen*, a 0-4-0WT to work the branch, rolling stock being hired from the SDR which worked the line.

Despite fish traffic in addition to the general services offered by the railway, expenditure exceeded income and in July 1870 Wolston was obliged to mortgage his engine as security. An accountant engaged by thoughtful

14XX class 0-4-2T No 1466 leaves Churston propelling the auto car to Brixham 25 July 1953. R.E.Toop

Brixham station circa 1910. A 0-6-0ST stands at the passenger platform. The goods shed is of timber. Most of the track consists of bridge rail on longitudinal sleepers. Notice on the right the old-fashioned heavily-weighted point lever as opposed to the more modern signal-lever type. Author's collection

friends to inspect the balance sheet, discovered that the SDR had failed to credit the Torbay & Brixham with terminal charges. The SDR would not accept this omission, so the Torbay & Brixham appealed to the Railway & Canal Commissioners who found in favour of the Brixham line. The SDR then retaliated by introducing an extravagant fee for the use of its Churston station. A further appeal to the Commissioners resulted in another decision in favour of the Torbay & Brixham, so the SDR was forced to pay £2,000.

4575 class 2-6-2T
No 5573 (83A
Newton Abbot) at
Brixham with a
permanent way
train, 7 August
1960. R.E.Toop

While these contentions were being examined, the GWR had taken over the SDR and worked the Brixham branch with GWR stock and the Torbay & Brixham's *Queen*. When she required maintenance, the GWR supplied a replacement. In July 1877 the GWR sold 0-4-0T No 2175 *Raven* to the Torbay & Brixham and proved suitable for conversion to standard gauge in 1892. *Raven* was sold to the Wantage Tramway in 1910 and cut up in 1919.

The Torbay & Brixham Railway was taken over by the GWR on 1 January 1883 and converted to standard gauge 20-23 May 1892. The branch closed to both passsengers and goods 13 May 1963.

Passenger trains to Brixham left from the bay platform at Churston. About half a mile short of the terminus were Air Ministry sidings opened 23 October 1940 and later used by the Ministry of Power. The station building at Brixham was constructed of timber. In addition to the good shed, a fish shed was provided. Fish formed an important traffic and until the branch's closure, left by rail almost daily. In 1950 the number of fish vans averaged from three to five daily.

Curiously, almost until closure, the branch time table showed an increasing number of trains. For example, the eighteen-eighties service of about nine trains each way daily increased to 17 in the nineteen-twenties and 25 in 1938. The final timetable offered 13 trains each way on weekdays.

Newton Abbot to Moretonhampstead

The broad gauge Moretonhampstead & South Devon Railway received its Act of Parliament 7 July 1862. The SDR required that all bridges be constructed to allow for doubling the line as it hoped eventually to reach

A Moretonhamp-
stead to Newton
Abbot train arrives
at Heathfield pre-
1916. On the left a
timber baulk road
serves Candy's
Great Western
Pottery, Brick &
Tile Works. The
gate indicates the
boundary of
railway and private
property. Author's
collection

LSWR territory at Okehampton. Part of the route followed the formation of
the Haytor Tramway, Devon's first permanent line. The Moretonhampstead
branch opened 4 July 1866 and was worked by the SDR which absorbed it
1 July 1872. The line was converted to standard gauge 20-23 May 1892. In
addition to other advantages, this conversion saved £144 annually on transfer
expenses at Heathfield with the Teign Valley Railway. The passenger service
was withdrawn from 2 March 1959 and Moretonhampstead closed to freight
traffic 6 April 1964, Bovey following 6 July 1970, but Heathfield remained
open to deal with china clay and oil.

Adjacent to the junction with the main line at Newton Abbot were power
station sidings and the goods depot for Newton Abbot. Teignbridge had clay
sidings and at Heathfield, Geest Industries Ltd had a private siding from
February 1961 until December 1975 and in June 1965 Gulf Oil sidings were
brought into use. Beyond were Bovey Granite and Bovey Pottery sidings.
Until the early nineteen-fifties, patients destined for Hawksmoor Sanatorium
arrived at Hawksmoor Halt (re-named Pullabrook 13 June 1955) and finished
the final leg of the journey by horse-drawn vehicle. Lustleigh station had a
camping coach. In 1931 the station was temporarily re-named Baskerville
for filming Conan Doyle's novel. It is believed that this was the first time a
talkie was made featuring a moving train. Another feature of Lustleigh station
was a small gravestone with the epitaph:

Beneath this stone and stretched out flat
Lies Jumbo, once our station cat.

The terminus at Moretonhampstead was 550ft above Newton Abbot.
The station platform was covered by a train shed. From October to March

A bevy of GWR charabancs at Bovey circa 1925. Left is No 238 registration T 7692 an AEC 3 ½ ton destined for Haytor Rocks; No 857, XY 2110 a Burford 30 cwt for Becky Falls and Manaton, while an unidentified vehicle, probably another Burford will go to Princetown. Two more charabancs stand beyond. Author's collection

Steam railmotor No 57 heads through the 1927 flood at Bovey Tracey. It was withdrawn that December. Author's collection

14XX class 0-4-2T No 1466 at Bovey Tracy with the 1.35pm to Newton Abbot 28 February 1959, the last day of passenger service. No 1466 is now preserved. Michael Jenkins

5101 class 2-6-2T No 4117 works the 2.15pm Newton Abbot to Moretonhampstead on 28 February 1959, the last day of passenger service. Michael Jenkins

5101 class 2-6-2T No 4117 north of Pullabrook Halt with the 2.15pm Newton Abbot to Moretonhampstead, 28 February 1959. Michael Jenkins

A Moretonhampstead to Newton Abbot train hauled by a 2-4-0T, at Lustleigh circa 1910. Land on the left would have allowed a second platform to be built. Author's collection

Lustleigh, renamed 'Baskerville' for the 1931 filming of Conan Doyle's novel. Author's collection

5101 class 2-6-2T No 4117 running round at Moretonhampstead after arrival with the 2.15pm from Newton Abbot 28 February 1959, the last day of passenger working. The prices on the posters advertising day returns available after 9.30am are: Torquay 3s 2d; Dawlish 3s 6d; Torre 2s 11d; Teignmouth 3s 1d and Paignton 3s 5d. Michael Jenkins

14XX class 0-4-2T No 1466 at Moretonhampstead after working the 12.50pm from Newton Abbot on 28 February 1959. No 1466 has been preserved. Michael Jenkins

14XX class 0-4-2T No 1466 (83A Newton Abbot) at Moretonhampstead. Author's collection

hampers of rabbits were despatched. After WW2 lignite was sent from the station in addition to the usual agricultural traffic. On 9 April 1906 the GWR operated a bus service to Chagford and from 12 July 1909 tours were run to Princetown and Dartmeet. The GWR opened the Manor House Hotel in 1930. It had been built in 1907 for Viscount Hambledon, head of W.H. Smith & Sons. As an hotel it had an 18-hole golf course within its grounds. Requisitioned as an army hospital 1940 until 1946, BR sold it in 1983.

In the years immediately preceding WW1 a through coach was run daily to and from Paddington. In 1922 half of the branch trains were through services from Kingswear, Paignton and Plymouth, that from Paignton using the corridor stock of the through Wolverhampton to Paignton service. One train terminating at Bovey was practically an express. Leaving Paignton, it

only called at Torquay and Torre en route, not even stopping at Newton Abbot.

Totnes to Ashburton

The Buckfastleigh, Totnes & South Devon Railway received its Act on 25 June 1864, a further Act of 26 May 1865 permitting an extension to Ashburton. The broad gauge line opened on 1 May 1872 was worked by the SDR. The branch was converted to standard gauge over the weekend of 21/22 May 1892. Unfortunately to reach Newton Abbot, the principal commercial centre for Ashburton, involved changing trains at Totnes, the 18¼ mile rail trip taking twice as long as the 7¼ mile 25-minute bus ride. The line closed to passengers 1 November 1958 and goods services were withdrawn on 7 September 1962.

Unusually, at Totnes no bay platform was provided for the branch train, which meant that the main line platforms had to be used and this could cause poor connections. Beyond Stretchford the GWR provided an iron ore siding, the mineral being taken to Totnes Quay. The train shed at Ashburton was almost identical to that at Moretonhampstead. When the woollen mills were working at full capacity, Buckfastleigh's goods revenue actually exceeded that of any SDR main line station. Four large cattle fairs were held at Ashburton annually and each required up to 90 cattle trucks.

14XX class 0-4-2T No 1470 arriving at Totnes with a train for Ashburton 5 August 1953. 5101 class 2-6-2T No 5150 with duty disc '2' (11.45am until 1.00am) waits outside the shed. R.E.Toop

14XX class 0-4-2T No 1470 at Staverton on 1 November 1958, the last day of passenger service. Author's collection

An ex-Devon Belle observation car at Staverton 17 August 1971. R.E.Toop

Steam railmotor No 30 at Buckfastleigh shortly before it was withdrawn in October 1935. Notice the advertisements fixed to the fence opposite the main platform. Author's collection

The Ashburton terminus seen from the station throat. The track is flat-bottomed. Author's collection

14XX class 0-4-2T No 1470, known locally as Bulliver, worked the branch for many years. Its name was probably a corruption of Bolivar, for in Kipling's *Ballad of Bolivar* one verse reads:

> Rocketing, her rivets loose, smoke stark white as snow,
> All the coals adrift adeck, half the rails below,
> Looking like a lobster pot, steering like a dray –
> Out we took the 'Boliver', out across the Bay.

Closure by BR was not the end of this line which runs through very picturesque scenery. It was taken over for preservation by the Dart Valley Light Railway (DVLR) and on 5 April 1969 the first passenger train on the re-opened line ran from Buckfastleigh to Totnes. Since 1971 the line was cut back to Buckfastleigh as land near Ashburton was required for improvements to the A38. The DVLR's headquarters were established at Buckfastleigh. Across the river from Totnes a station was set up at Littlehempston, the station building coming from Toller on the Bridport branch. In 1991 the name of the line was changed to the South Devon Railway.

Brent to Kingsbridge

The Kingsbridge & Salcombe Railway Act received Royal Assent 24 July 1882 and before completion, its powers passed to the GWR by an Act of 13 August 1888. Actually the line never reached Salcombe, though earthworks were completed to the far side of Batson Creek. The standard gauge line was opened to Kingsbridge 19 December 1893. In due course road competition was too great and the line closed to all traffic on 16 September 1963, the junction station at Brent remaining open until 5 October 1964.

Avonwick station, view Up, 2 August 1960. R.E.Toop

4575 class 2-6-2T No 5558 approaches Gara Bridge with the 12.24pm Brent to Kingsbridge, 16 May 1959. Michael Jenkins

The branch was in a superbly scenic location, indeed the GWR provided camping coaches at all three stations. The railway historian T.W.E. Roche believed it to be the ideal line for preservation and after successfully persuading local authorities to back him, walked out of the meeting to discover the track being lifted. It was to have been given the marketing title of 'The Primrose Line' and plans involved running trains for the local population in winter – it had proved invaluable during the harsh winter of 1962-3 – and for tourists in summer.

Loddiswell, view Up 2 August 1960. Camping coaches can be seen beyond the platform canopy. R.E.Toop

4575 class 2-6-2T No 5525 with the 2.10pm Kingsbridge to Brent about to enter the 638yd long Sorley Tunnel, 12 August 1961. R.E.Toop

Coaches at
Kingsbridge 2
August 1960. In the
bay platform
beyond the station
building is a
luggage van for
Passengers Luggage
in Advance.
R.E.Toop

The junction with the main line was at Brent where branch trains used the outer face of the Down island platform. Leaving the station, the line curved down a down gradient of 1 in 50, reaching the Avon and following its course.

The first station was Avonwick and like all stations on the branch was designed by William Clarke whose simple, but attractive designs were used by other branch lines, including the Bristol & North Somerset Railway between Bristol and Radstock where the first of his designs appeared. The Kingsbridge & Salcombe Railway was the last new line for which he was responsible.

Onwards to Gara Bridge through a thickly wooded valley, the Avon was crossed no less than ten times. Loddiswell station was unfortunately half a mile from the village and 200ft below, so this deterred passengers returning from shopping trips. The 638yd long Sorley Tunnel was passed before reaching the terminus at Kingsbridge. During WW2 an engine driver spotted an approaching German aircraft, opened his regulator fully and reached the safety of Sorley Tunnel, thus averting the attack. Through coaches from Paddington were run on summer Saturdays. The last regular steam-hauled passenger train ran on 10 April 1961 and the last steam-hauled freight on 11 July 1962.

When Kingsbridge station was enlarged circa 1926, the work was carried out in Clarke's style. In addition to the usual goods shed was a two-coach-long corrugated iron carriage shed. The line was particularly busy with special trains in the weeks up to D-Day as the coast at Slapton, being rather similar to the Normandy beaches, was used for training purposes. One interesting item of traffic was that circa 1910, thrice weekly a rabbit van left Kingsbridge and its hampers transferred at Bristol for the Midland Railway and the London & North Western Railway.

The GWR inaugurated a bus service between Kingsbridge and Salcombe on 21 July 1909 and operated it until 31 December 1928 when it was taken over by the Western National Omnibus Co. This was in competition with the existing ferry which, with its direct route, took only a little longer and was pleasanter. In 1927 the GWR bought out the ferry steamers to eliminate competition, and ran the ferry service until 1934.

During the last week that the branch was open, a steam-hauled four-coach restaurant car special left Brent. Drinks were running low, so an emergency stop was made at Avonwick to purchase two cases of whisky from the nearby public house. The train stopped at Gara Bridge for dinner . A sweepstake was held and the winner pulled the communication cord. This was done at Topsham level crossing between Gara Bridge and Loddiswell. Passengers gave the crossing keeper a glass of whisky and a motorist held up at the crossing was also invited to climb on the train to celebrate. He travelled to Kingsbridge and was deposited on the return journey.

Tavistock Junction to Launceston

The broad gauge Tavistock & South Devon Railway Act received Royal Assent 24 July 1854, opening to passenger traffic on 22 June 1859 and to goods 1 February 1860. The line was leased to the SDR which absorbed it 1 July 1865.

On 30 July 1862 the Launceston & South Devon Railway Act received Royal Assent for constructing a line linking Launceston with the proposed railway at Tavistock. The broad gauge line opened to passenger traffic 1 July 1865, goods traffic following on 21 August 1865. The company amalgamated with the SDR 31 December 1873.

To enable the standard gauge LSWR to use the line between Lydford and Plymouth, a third rail was added at a cost of £86,000. The first LSWR train ran over it on 17 May 1876 making the former branch line part of the LSWR's main line to Plymouth. In due course on 2 June 1890 the LSWR opened its own parallel track and the Lydford to Plymouth section of the Launceston line reverted to branch status. The Launceston to Tavistock length was converted to standard gauge 20 to 23 May 1892.

During WW2 measures were taken to provide alternative routes in the event of enemy action closing a line. One such was a chord line laid at Launceston

A train at Marsh Mills circa 1900; the first two coaches were built circa 1875. Gauge conversion gave a wide space between the tracks. Author's collection

At Yelverton 22 September 1955, 64XX class 0-6-0PT No 6421, right, works the Tavistock auto train while 45XX class 2-6-2T No 4542 heads the Princetown mixed train, left. Author's collection

Adams 0-6-0 No 442 derailed 18 November 1885. The track in the top left hand corner is mixed gauge. Author's collection

A 3521 class 4-4-0 entering Horrabridge circa 1905 with an Up train of varied coaching stock. Author's collection

A 57XX class 0-6-0PT at Tavistock circa 1946. Author's collection

The ex-GWR platforms at Lydford, view towards Plymouth circa 1963. Unusually the LSWR pattern signal box bears a GWR cast iron nameplate. The SR platforms are spanned by the concrete footbridge. Lens of Sutton

A 2-6-2T approaches Liddaton Halt 21 May 1951. The halt opened 4 May 1938. Author's collection

A 3521 class 4-4-0 leaves Coryton circa 1905 with a train from Launceston. New sleepers and chairs are stacked in the foreground. Author's collection

A goods train on the Up line at Lifton circa 1932. Four vans stand beside the Ambrosia milk factory. Notice the crossing keeper's cabin beyond the level crossing. Author's collection

between the GWR and the SR to offer either company another route Plymouth to Cornwall.

The Plymouth to Tavistock section enjoyed a significant commuter traffic until petrol rationing was abolished in 1950. From then until withdrawal on Saturday 29 December 1962, a single auto trailer sufficed. As a result of a severe blizzard, the last scheduled trains were cancelled and even the earlier ones were unable to complete the journey that day. The 7.10pm from Tavistock South, which proved to be the last passenger-carrying train over the branch, did not arrive at Plymouth until the afternoon of Sunday 30 December 1962.

Marsh Mills to Tavistock South, and Lifton to Launceston were closed completely on 31 December 1962. On 7 September 1964 Tavistock South to Lydford was closed and Lifton to Launceston re-opened, though only for a brief time, as Lydford to Launceston closed finally 28 February 1966.

The branch left the main line at Tavistock Junction and passed Marsh Mills where a station opened in 1861. Plym Bridge Platform opened 1 May 1906 and beyond were the 130yd long Cann Viaduct, the 117yd Riverford Viaduct, the 159yd Bickleigh Viaduct and the 171yd Ham Green Viaduct. Shaugh Bridge Platform opened 19 October 1907 and beyond was the 307yd long tunnel. Clearbrook Halt opened 29 October 1928. Yelverton, forming a junction with the Princetown branch, opened 1 May 1885. To the north was a 641yd long tunnel. Until Yelverton was built, Horrabridge acted as the junction station. Beyond were the 111yd long Magpie Viaduct, the 367yd Walkham Viaduct and the 374yd Grenofen Tunnel. Whitchurch Down Platform opened 1 September 1906. Tavistock station had a train shed covering its platforms. South of Mary Tavy the GWR passed below the

LSWR. At Lydford the GWR and LSWR stations were adjacent and from 8 January 1917 the signal box had two frames: that on the west side for the GWR and on the east for the LSWR. Liddaton Halt opened 4 April 1938. In 1965 an average of 16 container loads of rice pudding left Lifton daily. Three miles west of Lifton the line crossed into Cornwall where the branch terminated at Launceston.

On 27 February 1981 the Plym Valley Railway was incorporated to relay and work track north of Marsh Mills.

Yelverton to Princetown

An Act of 2 July 1819 authorised the 4ft 6in gauge Plymouth & Dartmoor Railway to link the Princetown stone quarries with Sutton Pool, Plymouth. The horse-worked tramway, using cast iron edge rails rather than the granite of the Haytor line, opened throughout in 1826. Apart from carrying stone to Plymouth, it drew coal, lime and timber in the reverse direction. Some passengers were carried, though this traffic was light. In 1850 Prince Albert proposed that the old prisoner-of-war barracks at Princetown be converted into a convict prison.

The amount of traffic then demanded better communication than a horse tramway, so a railway was authorised on 13 August 1878, much of the route following the course of the tramway which was purchased. The new line opened 11 August 1883 and although worked by it, was not absorbed by the GWR until 1 January 1922. With the development of road traffic the line closed completely 5 March 1956.

It was a difficult line to operate as 9½ of the 10½ miles were on a gradient of 1 in 40, curves causing friction and adding to working difficulties. The problem was eased by an apparatus which used steam to spray coolant on the rails in front of the leading wheels of the 44XX class 2-6-2Ts used. The system was cunningly designed so that it fed only the outer rail on a curve and

At Yelverton gravity was used to run the engine round the Princetown branch train. After arrival, the engine propelled the coaches up the branch, then uncoupled and ran into the loop. The guard released the coaches' brakes and so rolled them back to the platform behind the photographer. The engine then drifted down out of the loop and coupled to the coaches ready for the next trip. Note the check rails on the severe curve. Author's collection

A 1901 class 0-6-0ST snowed up on the Princetown branch. Author's collection

Dousland seen from a train. The coach is an ex-LMS vehicle. The signal box on the platform opened in 1915. Lens of Sutton

44XX class 2-6-2T No 4402 at Princetown September 1931. To the left of the smoke box can be seen a wheel-flange lubrication apparatus intended to ease the engine round the branch's severe curves. The system was economically powered by a Westinghouse pump and air reservoir from an ex-Railway Operating Division 2-8-0. The device was unsuccessful as the lubrication caused the driving wheels to slip. Author's collection

cut off completely when on straight track. Locomotives normally faced Princetown in order to keep the firebox crown covered with water when climbing and thus avoid melting the fusible plug.

Although the branch was 10½ miles long, the direct distance was less than six miles. Burrator Halt opened 14 February 1924 as an unadvertised workmen's platform but was made available to the general public 18 May 1925. Ingra Halt opened 2 March 1936, was probably unique in that it displayed a snake warning notice. King Tor Halt opened 2 April 1928. At 1,372ft above sea level, Princetown station was the highest in England so it is not surprising that despite its population of only 2,000, it received an average of four wagons of coal daily. A camping coach was stabled there.

The Yealmpton Branch

The Plymouth & Dartmoor Railway Act of 17 August 1894 authorised the GWR to construct a branch to Yealmpton. It opened to passengers 17 January 1898 and to goods a day later. It was an interesting line as the GWR could only reach it by running over LSWR metals. Bus competition caused

Diesel-mechanical D2229 at Plymstock. Built by Drewry it was equipped with a 204bhp Gardner engine and five speed epicyclic gearbox. No 2229 is now preserved. Notice the gradient post beneath the station name board. Lens of Sutton

An unusual station sign at Yealmpton, 1953. Author's collection

the line to close to passengers as early as 7 July 1930. Due to wartime conditions when some Plymouth residents were living in the country to escape bombing, or because their homes had been destroyed, the branch was re-opened for a workmen's service 21 July 1941 and to the general public 3 November 1941. Passenger services continued until 7 November 1947 and goods traffic was withdrawn 29 February 1960.

GWR trains departed from Plymouth Millbay, joined the LSWR at Cattewater Junction and used the Turnchapel branch (see page 147) to Plymstock. All the branch stations had a single platform, except for Plymstock which also had one serving the LSWR. Yealmpton station was designed as a through, rather than terminal station, as originally an extension to Modbury was planned, From 2 May 1904 a GWR bus linked Modbury with Yealmpton.

The Millbay Docks Branch

The Plymouth Great Western Dock Company was incorporated 18 August 1846 to construct docks and a broad gauge rail connection. An Act of 1874 enabled the three broad gauge companies, the GWR, B&E and SDR to take

over the company. On 16 June 1878 the branch was converted to mixed gauge, standard gauge wagons being worked from North Road by broad gauge locomotives.

To speed ocean mails, GWR tenders collected mail sacks from liners, carried them to Millbay where they were transferred to train and thence onward to Bristol and Paddington. From 1893 some passengers also used this route. Initially special passenger trains were run for each liner, but later, economies demanded a minimum of 25 first class passengers or their equivalent in mixed classes. Speed was important: a train left within 30 minutes of a tender arriving. To utilise the tenders when not serving liners, excursion trips were run to Eddystone Lighthouse.

The LSWR operated a rival service to meet liners. To avoid expensive competition, the LSWR withdrew from shipping activities at Plymouth and the GWR abandoned its Plymouth to Brest ferry.

In the late thirties, Plymouth dealt with an average of 500 liners annually, landing 30,000 to 40,000 passengers. In November 1961 French Line vessels ceased using Plymouth, so one of the two tenders was withdrawn and complete boat trains were discontinued. All rail traffic to the docks was withdrawn 30 June 1971 and the branch closed.

6 The London & South Western Railway Route to Plymouth

A horse bus outside Axminster station circa 1905. The chimney stacks are unusually tall. Author's collection

THE MAIN LSWR line entered Devon east of Axminster and ran to Exeter Queen Street. It was built under the Exeter & Yeovil Railway Act of 21 July 1856. Its engineer was Joseph Locke who bought the manor of Honiton and was the town's MP. The line opened to passengers 18 July 1860 and to goods 1 September 1860. When planning the route Locke avoided costly earthworks and tried to serve as many market towns as possible. Unfortunately the line passed across the grain of the country, making the

course switchback and this had its effect on the locomotive department. It used specially designed engines with driving wheels at least six inches smaller than those employed between London and Salisbury. These smaller wheeled engine were much better at climbing. The usual way of working expresses between Salisbury and Exeter was to tear down a bank as fast as possible to get plenty of impetus to climb the next. As the line was inland, branches were run to seaside watering places – Lyme Regis, Seaton, Sidmouth, Budleigh Salterton and Exmouth. The double track main line was singled 11 June 1967 as an economy measure.

Axminster, like many of the stations on the LSWR, was designed by William Tite who had a penchant for tall, steeply-pitched roofs combined with tall chimneys. To cater for the Lyme Regis branch, a bay platform was

S15 class 4-6-0 No 30841 leaves Axminster 2 August 1958. South Western Circle Wessex collection

King Arthur class 4-6-0 No 30755 *The Red Knight* waits at Seaton Junction circa 1950 for the up 'Devon Belle' to pass hauled by Merchant Navy class Pacific No 35009 *Shaw Savill*. Lens of Sutton

Diesel-electric No 10203 passes Seaton Junction with the 4.30pm Exeter Central to Waterloo 14 June 1954. Notice the tall signals are repeated at a lower level so that they can be easily seen from either side of the footbridge. S.W.Baker

made at the west end of the Up platform. The nearby carpet factory offered considerable traffic to the LSWR.

Seaton Junction, originally named Colyton, then Colyton Junction, had bay platform constructed at the west end of the down platform for use by branch trains. In 1927-8 the station was rebuilt to offer two platform and two through roads. The large adjacent dairy placed significant traffic on the railway. In 1935 the SR constructed a pipe line to carry water from springs near Honiton Tunnel to the Express Dairies at Seaton Junction. It also supplied the station and saved a porter many hours of hard pumping. The station and several others on this route, closed to passenger traffic 7 March 1966.

The line climbed at 1 in 80 to Honiton Tunnel 1,345yd in length, the longest on the LSWR and dead straight. Boring it resulted in only one death when a rock fell and crushed a man. It was lined with between 11 and 12 million bricks.

During WW2 Honiton was the railhead for an army camp at Heathfield and airfields at Dunkeswell and Upottery. Initially this involved the station coping with wagons loaded with construction materials and then when completed, personnel and their nutritional and other requirements. Trains were used to and from Exeter for their recreation. Following the 1967 track singling leaving a long passing loop at Honiton, the Tite buildings were demolished as BR claimed that they were too expensive to maintain. They were replaced by austere brick and glass structures whose unattractiveness has been somewhat ameliorated by a tiled roof, a little easier on the eye than the original flat design.

Roundball Halt, half a mile west of Honiton, opened 22 September 1906 for use by the Territorial Army using the nearby rifle range. Never opened to the public, its removal was ordered in 1921. It is interesting to record that two miles west of Feniton the buildings of Lashbrook Farm had to be demolished as they lay on the route of the railway. The replacement house was built in the Tite style of architecture, while the barns resembled his goods sheds.

N15 class 4-6-0 No 457 at Sidmouth Junction with a Down train in the 1920s. Freda Clayton

Sidmouth Junction opened as Feniton, became Ottery & Sidmouth Road, then Feniton for Ottery St Mary, then Ottery Road before its renaming as Sidmouth Junction. It closed to passengers when services were withdrawn from the Sidmouth branch 6 March 1967. It reopened as Feniton 3 May 1971 following pressure from residents of a new housing estate.

Whimple still has a monkey puzzle tree on the platform. About 1930 Whiteway's cyder – they use this spelling – factory was erected and in 1950 up

West Country class Pacific No 21C113 (later named *Okehampton*), with an Up train at Sidmouth Junction. A train to Sidmouth stands in the bay platform, left. Lens of Sutton

A female booking clerk date stamps a ticket at Sidmouth Junction in 1941. Author's collection

A notice at Feniton station 18 July 1989. Author

COMING BACK?

WHEN RETURNING TO FENITON, PLEASE BE

PREPARED TO ALIGHT FROM THE SECOND COACH

FROM THE FRONT OF THE TRAIN (OR A DOOR IMMEDIATELY

ADJACENT TO IT). THIS IS TO AVOID BEING 'OFF

THE PLATFORM' ON ARRIVAL HERE.

to 20 wagons loaded with cyder were despatched daily. Its employees swelled the passenger traffic figures. Whiteway's purchased three-monthly season tickets for their workers and gave them free. Written by hand, they were a day's work for a booking clerk. In the nineteen-sixties, stone from Rockbere Hill Quarry was sent from Whimple to Portishead for use by Albright & Wilson. In November 1992, as goods traffic had ceased, the former Down platform was demolished and the single line slewed to the former Up platform to avoid passengers having to use the footbridge. A new passenger shelter was provided and the reconstructed station opened 19 February 1993. At one time the following conversation took place in the Whimple booking office. 'I want a return, please.' 'Where to?' 'Back here of course!'

Broad Clyst was interesting for its unusual, though not unique water tower surmounted by a tower supporting a wind-powered wheel to operate

the pump. This feature disappeared in the nineteen-fifties when the pump was electrified. Until it was closed in 1964, an engineer's yard at Broad Clyst assembled track panels ready for relaying. Invalid motor tricycles were despatched by rail from the station.

The line to Exeter had been in use for 11 years before Pinhoe station opened 30 October 1871. It did not receive a Tite building. Closed to passengers 7 March 1966 it reopened 16 May 1983 and is at the commencement of the double track onwards to Exeter. Metal shelters stand on both platforms. When Network Southeast was set up in June 1986, Whimple formed its most westerly station, though later the boundary was extended to include Exeter Central.

Merchant Navy class Pacific No 21C8 *Orient Line* heads the Down 'Devon Belle' near Talaton, 20 September 1948. Pursey Short

Grain silo and brick siding, Pinhoe, view west 8 August 1984. Author

Steam crane at Pinhoe hoisting the main girder of a new concrete footbridge. Author's collection

Exmouth Junction locomotive shed 4 October 1952: West Country class Pacific No 34029 *Lundy* and 02 class 0-4-4T No S224. Colin Roberts

Whipton Bridge Halt opened 26 January 1906 with the inauguration of steam rail motor service between Exeter and Honiton. It closed 1 January 1923 due to relatively expensive repairs being required and insufficient traffic to justify the cost.

The interior of the carriage and wagon shop at Exmouth Junction, 7 August 1984. Author

Exmouth Junction had no passenger station, but a large engine shed opened there on 3 November 1887 in cheap and fireproof corrugated iron, but not long-lasting. It was rebuilt in concrete in 1927. The number of locomotives allocated varied over the years, but was approximately 110. They consumed about 300 tons of coal daily. Its repair shop contained lathes, slotting, shaping, planning and drilling machines, while locomotives parts were despatched to outlying sheds. The depot closed 6 March 1967. West of the engine shed was a gas works to supply fuel for lighting passenger coaches. Nearby was a carriage and wagon repair shed. Following privatisation this was leased to Messrs Jarvis, but the shops closed in 2004.

In 1913 the LSWR opened a concrete works to manufacture such items as concrete fencing, foot bridges, mile and gradient posts and station name

The concrete depot at Exmouth Junction circa 1928, its roof having been re-cycled from Exeter Queen Street station. Author's collection

Mount Pleasant Road Halt, Exeter circa 1924. The locomotive, believed to be T9 class 4-4-0 No 716, has emerged from the 263yd long Black Boy Tunnel with a train to Waterloo. This halt, opened in 1906, closed 2 January 1928. The distant signal arm is red and white, rather than the yellow and black of later years. Author's collection

boards. Stone chippings were supplied by Meldon Quarry and sand raised from the Taw-Torridge estuary was brought by rail from Fremington. In 1961 100 tons of concrete castings were made daily.

Mount Pleasant Road Halt opened 26 January 1906 and closed 2 January 1928, was sited at the east portal of the 263yd long Black Boy Tunnel. Lions Holt Halt also opened 26 January 1906, but was renamed St James' Park Halt 7 October 1946 to reflect the name of the nearby football ground.

Exeter Queen Street was spanned by a train shed. W. Hinde wrote that between 1879 and 1896 '...to keep the old building on the down side together,

West Country class Pacific No 34092 *City of Wells* heads a ballast train from Meldon Quarry through St James' Park Halt, 18 April 1964. No 34092 has been preserved. R.A.Lumber

Exeter Queen Street from the east circa 1905. Author's collection

LSWR Thornycroft bus, registration AA 2236, on the Chagford route, outside Exeter Queen Street station circa 1908.
John Cummings

The exterior of
Exeter Central 30
October 1966 with
names of some
destinations on the
awning.
R.A.Lumber

one or two carpenters were employed almost daily to repair the rotten state which presented itself. I have often said I believe I saw the down side rebuilt with wood'. On 1 July 1933 a new totally rebuilt station was opened as Exeter Central. For many years Exeter lacked a crematorium, so a van was attached to a Plymouth train for the coffin, while the mourners occupied reserved seats in a coach. In 1959 about two million passengers passed through the booking hall. A workforce of 1,500 was employed at Central and Exmouth Junction earning just over £1m annually. The last regular steam-hauled train to Exeter Central ran on 29 November 1965.

Beyond the station the line descended at 1 in 37 to Exeter St David's, passing through the curved 184yd long St David's Tunnel. This extension from Queen Street opened 1 February 1862. It was not unknown for an Up train to have four engines – two at the front and two in the rear. Although the Salisbury to Exeter line was well-used on summer Saturdays, on other days traffic was light, and it saw little freight. Principal non-passenger traffic was

E1R class 0-6-2T
No 32697 assists
the 11.00am
Plymouth to
Brighton up the 1
in 37 bank from
Exeter St David's to
Exeter Central, 30
July 1959.
R.A.Lumber

for railway needs: ballast from Meldon and coal for locomotives. With dieselisation, express services were replaced by semi-fast trains Waterloo to Exeter because it was believed that passengers desiring an express service could travel from Paddington via Taunton.

The line had been used by two named trains: the Atlantic Coast Express which began in 1927 and was the most multi-portioned train in England, having sections for Ilfracombe, Torrington, Padstow, Bude, Plymouth, Exmouth, Sidmouth and one coach for stations between Salisbury and Seaton. In addition it carried restaurant and kitchen cars. It frequently reached 80mph or over. On 16 June 1947 the Devon Belle was inaugurated, with six Pullman cars for Ilfracombe and four for Plymouth; an observation car tailed the Ilfracombe portion. Lacking sufficient patronage this train was withdrawn at the end of the 1954 summer time table.

The LSWR inaugurated a bus service from Exeter Queen Street to Chagford 1 June 1904 using petrol-driven Milnes-Daimler vehicles. The service was withdrawn 30 September 1904 but resumed 2 June 1905 using two Clarkson steam buses maintained, naturally enough, at the Exmouth Junction locomotive depot.

The LSWR strictly enforced the rule that dogs should not be taken into coaches. At Waterloo a lady entered a compartment with her Pekinese. The guard called her attention to a breach of regulations and offered to take the dog to his van. The lady refused to let him touch the animal and insisted on taking him personally. There she secured him to a box and gave the guard explicit instructions: 'Do not touch the dog'. She returned to her compartment.

After arriving at Queen Street she appeared at the van to claim her pet and failed to find him. She asked the guard where it was and received the reply: 'At Templecombe, ma'am. You told me not to touch him and as he was secured to a box labelled "Templecombe", when I put the box out there, the dog, of necessity, followed.'

The LSWR's Exeter to Plymouth line has a rather complicated history. Its first section was built by the Exeter & Crediton Railway under an Act of 21 July 1845. This was constructed as a broad gauge line, but before it could be opened, the LSWR purchased a majority shareholding. The Taw Vale Extension Railway, backed by the LSWR, relaid the Exeter & Crediton to standard gauge. This work having been done, the Railway Commissioners announced that it must be broad gauge. The Exeter & Crediton was therefore left unused until the spring of 1851 when one road was reconverted to broad gauge. The line opened ceremonially on 12 May 1851.

The line from Crediton to Coleford Junction was built by

The Exeter & Crediton Railway seal.

Luggage labels: St
Cyres, Crediton,
Yeoford Junction,
Copplestone,
Morchard Road,
Lapford.

the Taw Vale Extension Railway under its Act of 7 August 1846 for the
construction of a line from Crediton to Barnstaple. On 24 July 1851 a
further Act changed the company's name to the North Devon Railway &
Dock Company (NDR). This broad gauge line from Crediton to Fremington
Pill was ceremonially opened on 12 July 1854. The NDR was amalgamated
with the LSWR 1 January 1865 and the Exeter & Crediton 26 June 1879.

From Coleford Junction the Okehampton Railway Act of 17 July 1862

North Devon
Railway timetable
November 1854
from The
Barnstaple &
Bideford
Miscellany &
North Devon
Advertiser,
23.11.1854

Charge for search, 2s. 6d; and if the Advertisement is found full
particulars of it may be had, agreeably to the following Scale:—
If advertised within 5 years £1 0 0 If advertised above 10 £3 0 0
,   above 5 years £2 0 0   above 20 £4 0 0
2s. 8d. must be remitted in postage stamps from the country.

Advertisement received for the London Gazette, and every Country and London Newspaper, &c.—The papers are regularly filed.—
The TIMES, GAZETTE, and other Papers, for upwards of one hundred
years past.—The Bank Unclaimed Dividend Book may be seen, one
the payment of One Shilling.—Wills inspected or Doctor's Commons at the cost of 10s., provided the date of the Testator decease is
given.

Agent for "Galignani's Messinger," PARIS.

AVERY & SON

Beg leave to inform their numerous Patrons and
the Public generally, that they continue to

Convey Goods by Railway,

TO LONDON, BRISTOL, & EXETER.

*Their LOW SCALE OF CHARGES, includes
collection and delivery of all Goods consigned to them*

Excellent spring vans for removing Furniture, valuable
Household Goods, Musical Instruments, and Glass, to and
from any part of the country, forwarded by road or Rail.
Every care and attention will be observed in loading and
delivery, and Goods well protected from weather, by
waterproof coverings. Carriage of heavy Goods to and from
the railway station, contracted for at low Rates per Ton.
Waggons daily to and from BIDEFORD, TORRINGTON,
ILFRACOMBE, and LINTON, &c.

ORDERS PUNCTUALLY ATTENDED TO.

The "EMERALD" Omnibus leaves the Angel
Inn every Morning for Ilfracombe, 8:45 a.m.,
returning from Ilfracombe for Barnstaple 5 p.m.

Parcels under 1 cwt., delivered in Ilfracombe at 6d. each,
and above 1 cwt., 8d. each, Passengers' Fares, 1s. each.

*** You must please to order by Luggage Train to
Barnstaple, care of AVERY and SON.*

*Choose for yourselves, which will you have? Free Trade
or Monopoly? AVERY and SON, or PRIDHAM and
LAKE?*

the whole of which they are offering at astonishingly
low prices.

Their present stock is Large, New, Choice & Cheap.

☞ Observe the address and enquire for—
R. HOWELL & Co's Noted Cheap Drapery Estab-
lishment, Square & Maiden Street.

WAR! WAR!! WAR!!!

Startling Predictions in Copestick's Prophetic

ALMANAC

For the Year 1855.————Price 3d.

The War with Russia was Predicted in Copestick's Alman-
ac for 1854; even when the Prime Minister of England in
his official seat, declared there would be no War.

*Remarkable Predictions are set forth upon the coming
events which at present agitate Europe; together
with a variety of Useful Information.*

Agent for Barnstaple,   J. JONES. 'Miscellany'
Office, Cross-Street

North Devon Railway.

November, 1854.

UP TRAINS.
From BARNSTAPLE: 7.30—10.0—12.30—6
SUNDAYS 8.30—6.30.

DOWN TRAINS.
From EXETER: 5.0—10.10—3.30—9.10.
SUNDAYS 6.10—4.0.

Coaches and Omnibuses run from the Station to Bideford
Instow, Torington, Lynton and Lynmouth, Ilfracombe via
Braunton, ditto via Marwood.

authorised a line to be worked by the LSWR. The single line to North Tawton was opened on 1 November 1865 and to Okehampton on 3 October 1871. An Act of 29 June 1865 changed the name of the company to the Devon & Cornwall Railway and allowed an extension to the SDR at Lydford (see page 79). The Devon & Cornwall Railway was absorbed into the LSWR in 1872 and the line opened to Lydford 12 October 1874.

Initially the LSWR trains to Plymouth used the GWR's Launceston branch south of Lydford, but this line with sharp curves and steep gradients did not make an ideal main line, the *Western Daily Mercury* commenting: 'Many passengers suffer considerably from the vibration caused by the sharp curve of the line'.

The Plymouth, Devonport & South Western Junction Railway (PDSWJR) supported by the LSWR, received an Act 25 August 1883 to construct a line from Devonport to Lydford. Difficulties were experienced raising the finance as it was an expensive line with viaducts totalling 1,324yd and tunnels 1,507yd. From 2 June 1890 LSWR trains ceased using the GWR line between Lydford and Plymouth, utilising the PDSWJR route to Devonport. On that day through coaches were run from Leeds via the Somerset & Dorset Joint Railway to Plymouth. As they left Leeds at 2.50am the service was unpopular and withdrawn at the end of September 1890. The LSWR's new route London to Plymouth was 16 miles shorter than that of the GWR. The PDSWJR was absorbed by the LSWR in 1922.

An Act of 19 July 1875 authorised the LSWR to construct a branch to a goods terminus at Plymouth Friary, thus obviating the need to terminate at the GWR's North Road station. This line opened 1 February 1878. Friary passenger station opened 1 July 1891 gave the LSWR its own terminus close to the city centre and obviated the need to terminate its trains at North Road. Friary closed to passengers 15 September 1958 when it and the goods yard was converted into Plymouth's main goods depot.

The LSWR's line to Plymouth left the B&E at Cowley Bridge Junction and crossed the 88yd long Cowley Viaduct. Due to the legacy of the broad

The standard gauge 2-4-0WT No 181 with a Down train at Crediton circa 1880. Notice the mixed gauge track and that on the Down road, the standard gauge changes from the platform side to the off side. Author's collection

Two Down trains at Yeoford circa 1910: that on the left is headed by a 4-4-0 and on the right by a 0-6-0. The sign at the end of the platform canopy reads 'Refreshments'; a 5-ton crane in the yard loads timber. Author's collection

gauge, stations on the line have their platforms set well apart. Crediton has a Brunel-type station and at one time a double footbridge – one for passengers within the ticket gates, and the other for ordinary pedestrian use when the level crossing gates were closed.

At Coleford Junction, a mile beyond Yeoford, the Barnstaple and Plymouth lines diverged. On 17 October 1971 the former double track became two parallel single lines: the Down line for Meldon Quarry and the Up line to Barnstaple.

The line between Coleford Junction and Meldon Junction had been doubled 16 May 1877. From Coleford Junction the line climbs at 1 in 97. West of Bow station the track is straight for four miles – a phenomenon on a

Hampers of dead rabbits at North Tawton circa 1905. Author's collection

British railway. Okehampton station was rebuilt in 1928. Although the through service ceased 6 May 1968 and the line Meldon Quarry to Bere Alston closed, due to trouble on the sea wall on the former GWR line, and in order to clear goods traffic, the line through Tavistock was re-opened for one train to pass. The Exeter to Okehampton passenger service continued until 5 June 1972, but after this date excursion traffic still continued. The station was reopened 24 May 1997 with six trains running from Exeter each way on Sundays, some through from Paignton and Exmouth. 15,000 passengers were carried during the first 18 weeks of operation. Sampford Courteney station was re-opened 23 May 2004.

In the early days of railways, ballast consisted of the best material available locally, such as gravel, chalk or crushed stone, often dug out when cuttings were made. As the weight and speed of trains increased, crushed stone ballast was found to be the only suitable material for mainline running. When the line was being constructed between Okehampton and Lydford, it was discovered that the rock in the cutting near the east end of Meldon Viaduct made particularly good track ballast, but it was not until 1897 that the LSWR purchased land to start its exploitation.

Initially stone was loaded directly into wagons standing on the Down main line, but as soon as sufficient space had been cleared, a crushing plant was erected. In addition to track ballast, the quarry provided lump stone for walling; washed aggregate for concrete; road stone chippings and dust for blanketing. Circa 1949 a pound of explosive yielded five to eight tons of stone. No charges were permitted to be fixed until Meldon Quarry signal box had assured the quarry operator than no train was approaching on the main line.

Traffic at the military dock, Okehampton, view towards Okehampton station. The officers' mounts would have travelled in the two horse boxes, while those of the lesser ranks utilised cattle wagons. Notice that the main line climbing towards Meldon is at a higher level than the sidings. Author's collection

G6 class 0-6-0T No DS3152 in Meldon Quarry locomotive shed. Lens of Sutton

Meldon Quarry
Halt circa 1963,
view Down. The
platforms are
unusually narrow
as they were only
used by railway
staff, not the
general public.
Lens of Sutton

At times the Meldon Quarry signalman had to erect blast screens over his
signal box windows. Meldon Quarry Halt , only one paving stone in width,
was used by the pay clerk and quarrymen's wives. It closed when the
passenger train service was withdrawn.

The imposing Meldon Viaduct has six spans of 85½ ft, a maximum height
of 130ft and is set on a 30 chain curve. It is one of the very few all-metal
viaducts in Great Britain. Beyond the viaduct was Meldon Junction where
the line to Halwill Junction and Plymouth part company.

From Bridestowe station about 750ft above sea level, the Rattlebrook
Peat Railway climbed to over 1,800ft. The bee line distance of 2½ miles was
almost six miles by rail, including a reversing point. The line worked by a
steam locomotive, was opened by the West of England Compressed Peat
Company in 1879, but the company failed the following year. The railway
passed through many hands and in the early nineteen-hundreds, gravity was
used for down trains and horses for those in the up direction. During WW1
a chemical works was established on Dartmoor using peat. A petrol driven

A 4-4-0 crosses
Meldon Viaduct.
Author's collection

An Exeter to Plymouth DMU leaves Lydford 27 April 1968; the former GWR line on the far right has been lifted. R.A.Lumber

truck carried building materials and machinery for the works, and also drew a standard gauge wagon. This truck carried workers on day and night shifts. This trolley was used for salvage work following the Armistice and the railway's dismantling in 1931-2.

Tavistock North is now a Grade II listed building. One day in January 1898 William Backwell caught the 5.50pm from Exeter, but when it arrived at Tavistock his second class compartment door was found open with him missing. A goods engine was sent back up the line with two men as look-outs. He was found near Wallabrook, just north of the town. William Backwell was in a serious condition and Ganger John Milford imaginatively used flags to bind his left leg 'with a skill that won the praise of the doctor and the coroner's jury'. The locomotive carried him to Tavistock where he died early next morning at the cottage hospital. How did he come to fall from the train? William was prone to sleep-walking and this occurred in the train.

Following the withdrawal in 1968 of passenger trains over most of the line, the section from Bere Alston to Plymouth was kept open and singled as part of the Calstock branch. Bere Alston to Plymouth was formerly in the Down direction, but with closure of the line north of Bere Alston it was redesignated Up.

DMU to Gunnislake at Bere Ferrers, 14 August 1969. R.A.Lumber

The LSWR station at Victoria Road, St Budeaux, view up. The train has three non-bogie passenger coaches and a guard's van at each end. Notice the long, covered walkway between the overbridge and the platform. Author's collection

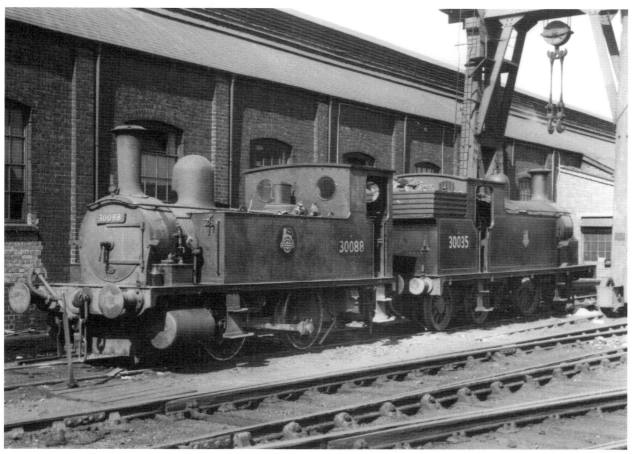

B4 class 0-4-0T No 30088 and M7 class 0-4-4T No 30035 at Plymouth Friary 13 May 1956. Notice the crane for lifting a locomotive. Rev Alan Newman

Devonport station circa 1910. Author's collection

Plymouth Friary in
LSWR days, view
towards the buffers.
Author's collection

South of Bere Ferrers the River Tavy Viaduct consists of eight bow-string girders, each spanning 111ft 4in, and nine masonry 50ft spans. Beyond Tamerton Foliot, which closed to passengers 10 September 1962, the seven span Tamerton Viaduct is crossed. Approaching St Budeaux the line twice passes below the GWR main line to Cornwall.

7 Branches from the London & South Western Railway Main Line

MOST OF the Axminster to Lyme Regis branch was in Devon, only crossing into Dorset prior to passing below the A3070, now B3165, about ½ mile before the terminus at Lyme Regis.

The Axminster & Lyme Regis Light Railway obtained its Light Railway Order on 15 June 1899. Arthur C Pain, appointed the line's engineer in 1872 had engineered the Culm Valley Railway (see page 54). On 10 April 1900 Baldry & Yerburgh's tender for building the line was signed and all shares taken by 5 July 1900.

0415 class 4-4-2T No 30583 leaves Axminster for Lyme Regis circa 1958; it has steam to spare. A cattle pen is to the right of the locomotive. R.J.Cannon

0145 class 4-4-2T No 30583 and No 50584 head a Down train at Combpyne. No 50583 is preserved. A camping coach stands in the siding, left, which until 12 August 1921, was a loop. The track is receiving attention. Author's collection

Combpyne circa 1936, view towards Lyme Regis. Notice the Express Dairy milk churns. Lens of Sutton

To enable the line to be constructed as cheaply as possible, it followed a sinuous course, the major engineering feature being Cannington Viaduct 203yd in length composed of ten arches. The structure was built of concrete, an aerial ropeway carrying the material to where it was required. In February 1902 frost caused work to be stopped for 14 days, while another problem developed when the contractors' locomotive being hauled to the site, jammed between two banks of a narrow lane near Trill.

Anticipating opening on 1 June, the Board of Trade inspection was fixed for 18 May 1903, but this notice had to be withdrawn when heavy rain caused a serious subsidence at the western end of the viaduct. To strengthen it, two arches, one above the other, were built within arch No 3. As the railway could not be used from 1 June, the LSWR arranged for a horse omnibus to make trips between Lyme and Axminster connecting with main line trains. This bus took 50 minutes in each direction, fares being two shillings inside and sixpence outside. Through third class tickets were issued from Lyme to London and vice versa for 13 shillings. The work of strengthening the viaduct proceeded quickly and the first train ran on 24 August 1903; one train having no less than 13 coaches was hauled by two engines. All were subject to a limit of 15mph over the viaduct.

The LSWR which had worked the line from the beginning, took over the local company on 1 January 1907. The following year it is recorded that 60,000 passengers, 1,900 parcels and 8,000 tons of goods travelled over the line, particularly heavy traffic being experienced that year, as from January to June sightseers came to view the burning cliff.

As the branch was built as a light railway, no signals were erected, so telephones were used to warn station when a train had left. An overall speed limit of 25mph was enforced, with a lower limit to 10mph around curves of less than 9 chains radius. The LSWR installed signals in July 1906, but the wheel turned full circle when on 27 March 1960 'one train working' was introduced by BR, all signals being removed.

Although busy on summer Saturdays, road transport took traffic from the railway and by 1952 the average number of passengers on a train worked out at 2½ in winter and 7 in summer. Final trains ran on 29 November 1965 and as stocks of Lyme Regis to Axminster day returns were exhausted, adults were issued with two child's tickets.

The opening of the branch posed a problem for Dugald Drummond, the LSWR locomotive engineer. The company's existing engines were thought to be unsuitable for the 9 chain radius curves and exceeded the weight restrictions. He contemplated building two special engines, but then decided on the cheaper solution of buying two second-hand 'Terrier' 0-6-0 tank engines from the London, Brighton & South Coast Railway. They proved to be insufficiently powerful for the heavy summer traffic and suffered from excessive tyre wear. One of these engines was sold to the Freshwater,

Yarmouth & Newport Railway on the Isle of Wight, later returning to the mainland to work the Hayling Island service. Restored as LBSCR *Newington* in 1966, she was placed outside the inn 'The Hayling Billy' as an outsize pub sign. In 1979 the brewers, Whitbread Wessex donated her to the Wight Locomotive Society.

The 'Terriers' were replaced on the Lyme Regis branch by standard 'O2' class 0-4-4 tank engines which were made sufficiently light by the tanks and bunker being only partly filled. The 'O2s' were not a roaring success as they suffered from excessive flange wear and distorted frames. Eventually an Adams' '415' class 4-4-2 tank engine was tried with specially modified bogie to give greater side play and thereby ease the negotiation of severe curves in which the branch abounded. For almost 50 years this class had a monopoly of the line. In 1946, both engines, now the sole survivors of this class on the Southern Railway, needed heavy repairs. There was but one other engine of this class still extant, a locomotive sold by the LSWR to the Government General Salvage Depot at Sittingbourne in 1917 and purchased by the East Kent Railway two years later. Although it had lain derelict since 1939, it was in repairable condition, overhauled and put into SR service. Following extensive track renewals and re-aligning of curves in 1960, it was possible to use more modern locomotives and the Adams' tanks were withdrawn, but fortunately the Bluebell Railway preserved No 30583 – the one rescued from the East Kent Railway.

Seaton Junction to Seaton

The Seaton & Beer Railway Act was passed on 13 July 1863. The line opened on 16 March 1868 and unusually for the period, there were no celebrations. Worked by the LSWR it was taken over by that company on 3 January 1888. In 1936 the station building at Seaton, which was described as 'more in keeping with a farmhouse than a railway terminus', was replaced by a modern building in art deco style. Although well-used in summer, traffic in other seasons was light, so trains were withdrawn 7 March 1966.

This was not the end of the story as Modern Electric Tramways Limited which had operated narrow gauge double deck trams at Eastbourne, was seeking

Ex-London, Brighton & South Coast Railway D1 class 0-4-2T No B214 beside the water tank at Seaton circa 1931. The coaches are the 1914 gated stock, probably set No 373. To the left of the locomotive's chimney is the water tank gauge. The pointer standing near the base of the scale, indicates a full tank. Lens of Sutton

a new home. As the Seaton & District Electric Tramway Company it opened a 2ft 9in gauge line to Bobsworth Bridge (the return fare was a shilling) on 28 August 1970, power obtained from a battery trailer. It offered, and still offers, a delightful ride beside the estuary. The line was extended to the level crossing at Colyford 9 April 1971 and power from the overhead used on 23 September 1973. On 17 May 1975 the tramway was extended at Seaton to

The exterior of Seaton station rebuilt in 1936. The wet road reflects the posters. Lens of Sutton

Car No 8 leaves Colyford for Seaton 3 June 1976. The LSWR cast iron gentlemen's urinal can be seen immediately to the right of the car. Author

M7 class 0-4-4T No 30048 with an Up train pauses at Colyton circa 1960 to attach, or detach a van. The locomotive stands under a loading gauge. Notice the compressed air pump beside the smoke box for working the motor train equipment. Lens of Sutton

Ex-GWR 64XX class 0-6-0PT No 6412 (86A Newport) at Colyton, works the 14.20 Seaton to Seaton Junction 26 October 1963. No 6412 is now preserved. Notice the water tank at the far end of the platform. E. Wilmshurst

the car park in Harbour Road, while the northwards extension to Colyton opened on 8 March 1980.

The increased number of visitors to Colyton caused certain problems, and in 1980 the *Seaton News,* in connection with a parish council meeting at Colyton, reported: 'The council should write back to say the tram company should provide toilets and also point out that the flow of passengers was not seasonal…but all the year round'.

The Sidmouth Railway

The Act for building the Sidmouth Railway was passed on 29 June 1871 and the line opened 6 July 1874. Unusually, the celebrations were spread over four days. On Regatta Day, 8 July 1874, a 17 coach special train arrived double-headed. Worked by the LSWR it proved a very profitable branch and in 1894 the LSWR sought to purchase it but it remained independent until

02 class 0-4-4T No 182 enters Ottery St Mary with a nine coach train circa 1910. The photographer is receiving more attention than the train. Author's collection

The 17.42 Sidmouth to Sidmouth Junction arrives at Tipton St John's having just descended the incline. The lines to Budleigh Salterton and Exmouth are on the right. Author

Mr Lancaster Smith about to name West Country class Pacific No 21C110 *Sidmouth* at Sidmouth, 27 June 1946. Curtains conceal the nameplate. I. Broughton

The exterior of Sidmouth station circa 1905. Notice the canopy sheltering the entrance so that in wet weather passengers could step dry-shod to, or from, a carriage or bus. The rear of the engine shed can be seen on the left. Author's collection

15 November 1922. The 1963 Beeching Report threatened the line with closure and despite local efforts to retain it, the passenger service was withdrawn on 6 March 1967. Dieselisation had taken place on 4 November 1963.

Tipton St John's was a two-platform station and immediately to the south, the Exmouth and Sidmouth branches diverged. From Tipton the Sidmouth branch rose at 1 in 45 for two miles before descending to the terminus 200ft above sea level and ¾ mile from the beach. It is believed that this awkward position was deliberately chosen to discourage day trippers from lowering the tone of this select watering place.

T1 class 0-4-4T No 14 at Sidmouth circa 1928. Freda Clayton

Sidmouth in a bowl: a 1912 LSWR poster.

Following the closure of Sidmouth gas works, the site was used for converting Volkswagen vans, which came by train from Ramsgate to Sidmouth, into caravanettes by Devon Conversions.

Tipton St John's to Budleigh Salterton and Exmouth

The Budleigh Salterton Railway Act was passed 20 July 1894 granting powers to construct a line from Tipton St John's. Lucas & Aird the contractors, completed the task on 14 May 1897, six months ahead of schedule – a strong contrast to most railways which were usually opened later than the date projected. The LSWR absorbed the company on 1 January 1912.

The LSWR Act of 25 July 1898 authorised the extension of the line as the Exmouth & Salterton Railway. It was a costly line as it included a viaduct 352yd in length and 30ft high near Exmouth and also the ¾ mile long Knowle cutting. The formation was wide enough for a double line, but only single track was ever laid. The line opened on Whit Monday 1 June 1903.

The opening rendered the Exmouth to Budleigh Salterton horse bus redundant. Its fare structure was interesting. In winter it cost 9d to travel inside, sheltered from the elements and 6d outside. In summer one had the option of suffocating inside for 6d or enjoying the breezes for 9d.

Camping coaches converted from ex-LSWR suburban stock seen here at East Budleigh 29 June 1948; No 6 left and No 11 right. J.H. Aston

During the summer Budleigh Salterton despatched herring and shellfish, the former filling as much as four vans daily. In the nineteen-fifties up to 40,000 tons of stone containing silica were sent to Albright & Wilson, Portishead. After the cattle market on alternate Mondays, 20 to 25 cattle trucks were despatched.

BR Standard Class 3 2-6-2T No 82010 (72A Exmouth Junction) at East Budleigh circa 1962. Lens of Sutton

Trains climbed at 1 in 50 to the summit at Knowle Cutting and then descended on the same gradient to Littleham and Exmouth. Latterly, the shunting spur at Littleham was used for stabling stock of the 1960 to 1962 summer Saturdays Cleethorpes to Exmouth train as on arrival it had to be kept until its return the following week. Because there was no room at

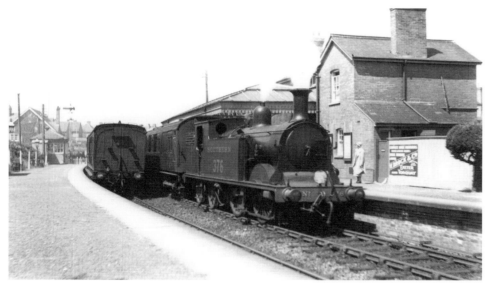

Exmouth, it was sent to Littleham. Southern and Eastern Region stock was used in alternate weeks.

The branch was mainly dieselised 4 November 1963 and services withdrawn 6 March 1967.

The Exeter & Exmouth Railway

The Exeter & Exmouth Railway Act was passed on 2 July 1855. It was to have been a broad gauge line, but when the standard gauge Yeovil & Exeter Railway proposed building a branch to Topsham, it was decided that the Exeter & Exmouth would complete the remainder to the same gauge. This change was authorised in an Act of 28 June 1858 while the LSWR received power to build the line to Topsham on 12 July 1858.

The ceremony of cutting the first sod proved surprising. It was a day of dual festivities as it coincided with the twenty-first birthday celebrations of the

Honourable Mark Rolle who was to perform the ceremony. He was two hours late arriving and then, either dying of hunger, or too overcome to undertake turning the first sod, he entered the Market House where the feast was to be held. The ceremony was eventually carried out by the company's chairman and in lifting the turf, he snapped the spade's handle. Undefeated, he lifted the sod with his hands and dropped it into the wheelbarrow.

The line opened on 1 May 1861, the first train comprising 11 coaches, while the second consisted of 19 coaches and required two engines and the third, also piloted, had 16 coaches. The company amalgamated with the LSWR 1 January 1866. Traffic increased sufficiently to warrant the Exmouth Junction to Topsham section being doubled 1 June 1908 when Polsloe Bridge and Clyst St Mary & Digby's halts were opened and served by the new Exeter to Topsham steam rail motor. The original timber platforms at Polsloe Bridge were replaced in 1927 by concrete components cast at the nearby SR concrete works. Clyst St Mary & Digby Halt closed 27 September 1948, but on 29 May 1995 Digby & Sowton station opened about 380yd to the south.

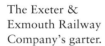

The Exeter & Exmouth Railway Company's garter.

Rear view of South Wales & West DMU No 150261 at Digby & Sowton, working the 11.54 Exmouth to Paignton, 11 March 1997. Author

Circa 1910 a 415 class 4-4-2T heads an Up train into Topsham station. Author's collection

The track was singled between Exmouth Junction and Topsham 3 to 5 February 1973, but Topsham station still retained its double track. At one time the station despatched considerable quantities of soft fruit and orchids. On 23 September 1861 the Topsham Quay branch, about half a mile in length, was opened. Due to the steep gradient of 1 in 38, in damp weather an engine could only manage to haul four loaded wagons. Two porters were required to walk beside a train on the incline and thrust sprags into the spokes should it run out of control. In the nineteen-twenties a special brake van was built which was required to be marshalled at the quay end of a train. An important commodity unloaded at Topsham Quay was guano. The quay branch closed in 1957.

A Down train hauled by a 02 class 0-4-4T arrives at Woodbury Road circa 1905. The station was renamed Exton 15 September 1958. Author's collection

Rear view of DMU set No 957 (Car No 51940 and No 52057), near Lympstone working the 10.30 Exmouth to Barnstaple 20 July 1989. The estuary of the River Exe can be seen beyond. Author

Beyond Topsham the picturesque line follows the estuary shore. On 3 May 1972 Lympstone Commando station was opened, the platform being re-cycled from Weston Milton halt near Weston super Mare. It is for the exclusive use of the Royal Marines.

The original station at Exmouth was economically created from two converted houses, but a new station was opened on 20 July 1924 and replaced

Lympstone with the estuary beyond, viewed circa 1904. The goods shed on the right was later converted to a waiting room. Posters form an interesting display. Author's collection

on 2 May 1976 by yet another. The station master of the first building met a tragic end. On 15 August 1871 when visiting the shop of a jeweller friend, he asked: 'Aren't you afraid of being robbed?' The jeweller replied: 'Oh no, I've got a very good friend here,' opened a drawer, removed what he believed to be an unloaded pistol, pointed it at the stationmaster and pulled the trigger. There was an explosion and the stationmaster dropped dead.

Beyond Exmouth station, an Act of 29 July 1864 authorised the construction of Exmouth Docks and siding. It carried such traffic as coal,

A busy scene at Exmouth circa 1960: on the left a train leaves for Sidmouth Junction double-headed by a Class 2 Ivatt 2-6-2T and a BR Standard Class 3 2-6-2T, while on the right BR Standard Class 3 2-6-2T sets off to Exeter Central. Author's collection

The exterior of Exmouth station 18 August 1978. The SR Estates' Department had an eye for business as it contained shops. Author

The exterior of Exmouth bus and railway stations 18 July 1989. Author

timber, grain, fertiliser, fish, cider apples and apple juice. This dock branch closed 2 December 1967. The rest of the branch had been almost completely dieselised on 9 September 1963 and is very much alive today.

DMU No 142019 at Morchard Road working the 12.33 Barnstaple to Exmouth, 8 August 1986. Author

Coleford Junction to Barnstaple

Continuing the story of the Taw Valley Extension Railway (page 99), the broad gauge service from Crediton to Bideford was withdrawn on 30 April 1877. The track was doubled between Crediton and Copplestone, but then an agreement with the GWR to pool receipts on competitive routes obviated the need to double the line Copplestone to Barnstaple. With the reduction in the line's use, it was singled Crediton to Copplestone 17 October 1971.

Lapford station was unusual in having its platforms staggered either side of an over bridge under which a slaughterhouse was situated in one of the arches. Crediton, Copplestone and Barnstaple also had LSWR slaughter houses. The Ambrosia Dried Milk Works were adjacent to the station.

South Molton Road station was nine miles from the town it purported to serve ('Road' was often added to the name of a station in effort to overcome untruthfulness), and due to complaints, following Nationalisation, it was renamed King's Nympton, though even this settlement was three miles distant,

The Up platform, Eggesford circa 1910. Author's collection

John Norman, Rail Operator II, at Eggesford with a full carrier of single line tablets to return to Barnstaple, 25 July 1994. Author

so this, too, should have had 'Road' added. Portsmouth Arms, opened in September 1855, was named after the public house, which in turn was called after the 4th Earl of Portsmouth of Eggesford House and a keen supporter of the railway.

West Country class Pacific No 34028 *Eddystone* (72A Exmouth Junction), at Portsmouth Arms circa 1958. No 34028 has been preserved. M.E.J.Deane

A broad gauge train at Barnstaple circa 1858, headed by 2-2-2 *Tite*, (formerly Bristol & Gloucester Railway No 5 *Gloucester* and subsequently Midland Railway No 261, then 361 and finally 461) built by Bury, Curtis & Kennedy in 1844. Notice the shunting horse, once a common sight on the railway. Author's collection

43XX class 2-6-0 No 6372 (83B Taunton) at Barnstaple Junction with the 16.10 to Taunton, 2 October 1963. R.A.Lumber

Class 2 2-6-2T No 41297 station pilot, and West Country class Pacific No 34106 *Lydford* at Barnstaple Junction 11 May 1963. R.E.Toop

A 1959 hand bill giving details of runabout tickets.

Barnstaple station became Barnstaple Junction from 20 July 1874 with the opening of the line to Ilfracombe. In its original state it had a single platform with a one-storey office building and two-storey station master's house. Its junction status in 1874 caused a Down platform to be built. In 1924 the hillside was excavated so that the Down platform could become an island. With the reduction in traffic following line closures, the former Up platform became the main platform and the track on the far side of the island platform lifted.

The Barnstaple & Ilfracombe Railway

Planning a railway to Ilfracombe was difficult as only three miles south of the town was a range of hills 800ft in height. The Barnstaple & Ilfracombe Railway Act was passed on 4 July 1870, but then there was a dearth of local subscribers. There were two main engineering features: the wrought iron viaduct over the Taw at Barnstaple which had 17 spans totalling 213yd and was constructed on a 7½ chain curve. The other feature was the 70yd long Ilfracombe Tunnel.

The line opened 20 July 1874. Passing over the Barnstaple Viaduct, one of the first trains exploded detonators making 'nervous parties fear the structure was snapping under them'. Meanwhile, by an Act of 16 July 1874 the LSWR acquired the Barnstaple & Ilfracombe Railway. Although land had been purchased for double track, the single line had been built in the centre and in several places doubling required the purchase of further land. Doubling was completed on 1 July 1891.

At the northern end of the single track viaduct was Barnstaple Quay station, (renamed Barnstaple Town July 1896), much closer to the town centre. 16 May 1898 a new Barnstaple Town station was opened 11 chains to the north also serving the Lynton & Barnstaple Railway (see page 142). Pottington Swing Bridge crossed the River Yeo and was slewed by rack and pinion gear. Beyond Pottington the track became double.

On summer Saturdays up to three engines could be seen at Braunton waiting to assist trains up the 1 in 40 gradient to Mortehoe. Ilfracombe station was situated on a hill above the town and 225ft above sea level. It was at the foot of a 1 in 36 gradient making some passengers nervous.

The seals of the Ilfracombe Railway, (abandoned in 1868) and the Barnstaple & Ilfracombe Railway companies.

Ilfracombe Goods 0-6-0 No 394 in Barnstaple shed October 1907. F.E.Box

West Country class Pacific No 34017 *Ilfracombe* crosses the River Taw near Barnstaple Town station with the Down 'Devon Belle', 1 August 1952. R.E.Toop

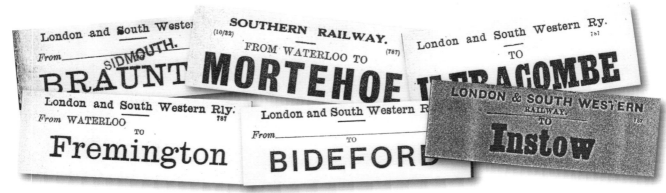

London and South Western

From SIDMOUTH.

BRAUNT

SOUTHERN RAILWAY.
(10/32)
FROM WATERLOO TO (787)

MORTEHOE

London and South Western Ry. 7b1

TO

ILFRACOMBE

London and South Western Rly. 787

From WATERLOO
TO
Fremington

London and South Western R

From
TO
BIDEFORD

LONDON & SOUTH WESTERN
RAILWAY.
TO
Instow
787

Luggage labels:
Braunton,
Mortehoe,
Ilfracombe,
Fremington, Instow,
Bideford.

A Barnstaple Town
luggage label
printed July 1939

SOUTHERN RAILWAY.
(7/39)   TO   Stock 787

BARNSTAPLE TOWN

Although the line enjoyed heavy traffic in summer, traffic in other seasons was too light to be economic. The line was worked by diesel multiple-units from 7 September 1964 and as a further economy measure singled 17 December 1967. All to no avail as it closed 5 October 1970.

View of Barnstaple
Town circa 1967
from the rear
window of a
departing Up
DMU. D. Payne

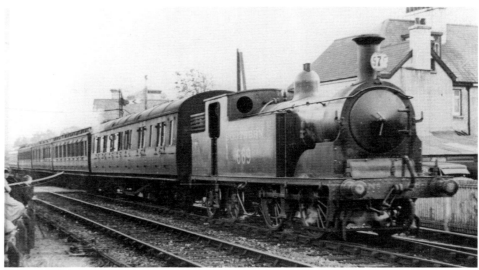

M7 class 0-4-4T
No 669 at
Braunton 28 July
1936 with a Bristol
to Ilfracombe train.
A through coach
from Paddington is
at the rear. S. Miles
Davey

BR Standard Class 4 2-6-4T No 80039 arrives at Mortehoe & Woolacombe 12 September 1965 with the Ilfracombe section of the Southern Counties Touring Society's 'Exeter Flyer'. Notice how the tracks fall out of sight on the gradient of 1 in 40, rather than disappear into the distance. R.E.Toop

N class 2-6-0 No 31837 ascends the 1 in 36 gradient out of Ilfracombe 6 August 1952. R.E.Toop

Ilfracombe station staff gather to celebrate Tom Short's last load, 21 November 1908. Van man Tom Short stands on the LSWR horse drawn parcels delivery van.
S. Hatchley collection

Ilfracombe Goods 0-6-0 No 283 leaves Ilfracombe circa 1907. A GWR coach in the siding emphasises the gradient of 1 in 36. The notice on the right reads: 'Speed 4 mph'.
F.E.Box

In July 1940 it was believed that beaches near the mouth of the Taw offered a potential site for a German invasion. An armoured train was brought to Barnstaple Junction, this being a convenient centre for patrolling the railway between Bideford and Braunton. A London, Midland & Scottish

Armoured train 'K', similar to the one which was used in North Devon in 1940. It is hauled by LNER F4 class 2-4-2T No 7573. Author's collection

Railway 20 ton steel-bodied locomotive coal wagon was fitted with a 6 pounder Hotchkiss Mk II gun, effective against a tank or armoured car at up to 800-1,000yd. Another compartment contained rifles and three Bren guns. One armoured wagon was for radio communication with headquarters. The train was hauled by ex-LNER 2-4-2T No 7077 also armoured and on loan to the War Department. The train's crew of about 31 was billeted at the Waverley Hotel, Joy Street, Barnstaple. The Army footplate men were required to pass the Southern Railway's rules and regulations test to the satisfaction of the district locomotive superintendent. When fears of invasion of the area subsided, the train left Barnstaple 20 April 1942.

Barnstaple to Halwill Junction

Although in later years the line between Barnstaple and Halwill Junction appeared to be one, it was actually an amalgam of several railways.

The Taw Vale Railway & Dock Company obtained an Act 21 July 1845 to construct docks at Fremington and a line to Barnstaple. It opened as a horse-worked line 25 April 1848, but with the opening of the NDR from Crediton to Barnstaple on 1 August 1854 broad gauge steam engines worked through to Fremington.

Bideford was determined not to be left off the railway map, so the Bideford Extension Railway Act was passed on 4 August 1853. The line opened ceremonially on 29 October 1855 and to the public on 2 November 1855.

The contractor, Thomas Brassey, leased both the NDR and the Bideford Extension and operated them as one. The LSWR took over both railways on 1 August 1862. The LSWR being a standard gauge company, converted the

Fremington circa 1930. On the quay, an Adams 4-4-0 heads a coal train which includes at least two LMS wagons. Braking could be a problem on a coal train hauled by an engine with this wheel arrangement. Beyond is a four-masted ship. Author's collection

line to mixed gauge. This was completed to Bideford on 2 March 1863, but one broad gauge train continued to run to Bideford daily until 1877.

Torrington was the next goal to be achieved, the authorising Act was passed 19 June 1865 and the line opened 18 July 1872. A few years later, the 3ft gauge Marland Light Railway was opened in 1880 to link the china clay pit at Petrockstow with the LSWR at Bideford. In addition to the average of 100 tons of clay carried daily, it also transported agricultural produce, bricks and coal. Workmen were carried in two ex-London horse trams and two open wagons covered and fitted with seats. The 135ft long timber-built Torrington Viaduct was so fragile that in order to lighten the axle load, the three Fletcher, Jennings & Co 0-4-0STs had their saddle tanks removed and placed on a trailing wagon.

The seal of the Bideford Extension Railway.

E1R class 0-6-2T No B94 at Instow circa 1930. The photographer's case and coat seem to be on the platform. Arthur Halls

The railway at Bideford circa 1852. Author's collection

M7 class 0-4-4T
No 30250 at
Bideford with a
Down train 5
August 1952.
R.E.Toop

A general view of
Torrington circa
1920 with the
passenger station,
left, and goods
shed, centre. Two
locomotives stand
outside the engine
shed located to the
left of the far end
of the passenger
train. On the right,
beyond the kissing
gate and between
the rakes of
standard gauge
wagons, can be
seen the transfer
siding with the 3ft
gauge wagons of
the Marland Light
Railway. Author's
collection

The final link to Halwill Junction was made by the North Devon &
Cornwall Junction Light Railway (NDCJLR) which, being a light railway, did
not need an expensive Act of Parliament, but merely a Light Railway Order
which was obtained 28 August 1914. It used part of the formation of the
Marland Light Railway. WW1 delayed its construction and it was not opened
until 27 July 1925. The track was composed economically of second hand
components and in 1980 some chairs still bore castings with 'LSWR 1900'.
Although nominally independent until Nationalisation in 1948, it had been
worked by the SR. It was the last major railway construction in the West of
England apart from the Westbury and Frome avoiding lines.

On 7 May 1963 a survey revealed that the average number of passengers
on a train from Barnstaple to Torrington was just over nine, while between
Torrington and Halwill Junction even one passenger on the two trains daily
was rare. Halwill Junction to Torrington closed to passengers 1 March 1965
and Torrington to Barnstaple 4 October 1965, though the latter closure was
temporary and trains re-instated 10 to 22 January 1968 when part of the
road bridge at Bideford collapsed.

On the 3ft gauge Marland Light Railway circa 1920, a Black Hawthorn 0-6-0ST crosses the timber viaduct at Torrington. The leading two coaches are ex-London horse trams, while the last two are converted open wagons. Author's collection

Ivatt Class 2 2-6-2T No 41298, now preserved, takes on water at Hatherleigh circa 1960. Lens of Sutton

Halwill Junction to Meeth closed to goods 1 March 1965 but clay traffic continued from Marland. By 1981 this consisted of one 57 tonne wagon daily. The branch closed 31 August 1982 when the cost of repairs to an underline bridge would have proved uneconomic. The clay was then taken by road to the railhead at Okehampton.

Fremington was an important port as annually 50,000 tons of locomotive coal from South Wales was landed there destined for LSWR sheds in the south west. Sand was despatched to Exmouth Junction concrete works. Outgoing traffic from the port was principally clay. The quay closed 30 March 1970. Instow signal box is now Grade II listed and from this station sugar beet and pit props were despatched.

Ivatt class 2 2-6-2T No 41298 at Meeth, crosses an ungated level crossing 14 August 1956. Part of a cattle grid can be seen to the left of the rear pony truck. The cast iron notice reading: 'Beware of Trains' is not too prominent. R.E.Toop

E1R class 0-6-2T No 2095 at the North Devon & Cornwall Junction Light Railway platform at Halwill Junction circa 1930. Author's collection

The original station at Bideford was closed and a replacement opened when the line was extended to Torrington. Torrington had the largest creamery in the West of England and in 1957 sent two million gallons of milk to London. South of the station the line crossed the Torridge on a nine-span steel girder bridge. The station at Hatherleigh was two miles from the town and a rail journey to Okehampton covered 20 miles, yet the road distance was only seven. Halwill Junction was originally called Beaworthy which was situated to the east. It was renamed Halwill Junction 1879 and by 1907 that name was adopted by the new settlement which had a cottage hospital and an hotel. At Halwill Junction the NDCJLR passenger trains used an independent shelterless platform.

In 1951 several motorists waited for a goods train to move past the closed level crossing gates at Halwill Junction. They waited for a considerable time. They then saw the fireman cross the street and climb on the engine. He had two ice creams, one for himself and one for his driver. The train then moved.

Meldon Junction to Halwill Junction

The first railway to arrive at Halwill Junction was the Devon & Cornwall Railway authorised by an Act of 7 July 1873 to build a line from Meldon Junction to Holsworthy. It opened on 20 January 1879 and the LSWR subsidised a horse bus onwards to Bude. Until the opening of the line, Bude's only communication with the outside world had been a thrice weekly coach to Okehampton. The LSWR took over the Devon & Cornwall Railway 30

N class 2-6-0 No 31849 at Ashbury 16 May 1964 working the 15.11 Bude to Okehampton. Notices of the proposal for withdrawing services are displayed on the notice board. R.A.Lumber

June 1879 and extended it to Bude on 11 August 1898. The last station on the line within the Devonshire boundary was Whitstone & Bridgerule. Despite dieselisation in September 1964, road competition caused passenger traffic to be withdrawn 3 October 1966, goods having finished 7 September 1964.

Ashbury station was situated 850ft above sea level and until closure, still used oil lamps. Halwill Junction was a busy station in the middle of nowhere, with four lines converging. The LSWR owned a slaughterhouse there and the War Department sidings were in use 1943-1963. Dunsland Cross had added to its station sign: 'Alight here for Shebbear College'. Holsworthy Viaduct of nine 50ft spans was notable for the fact that it was the first large concrete viaduct in Britain, pre-dating 'Concrete Bob' McAlpine's Glenfinnan Viaduct on the West Highland Extension in Scotland. Holsworthy was the site of yet another LSWR slaughterhouse. Beyond was the 176yd long Derriton Viaduct.

Halwill Junction to Whitstone & Bridgerule

An Act of 7 July 1873 authorised the construction of the Devon & Cornwall Railway between Halwill Junction and Holsworthy. It opened 20 January 1879 and was purchased by the LSWR 30 June 1879. This company extended the line to Whitstone & Bridgerule and Bude 11 August 1898. Road competition caused the branch to be closed to passenger traffic 3 October

N class 2-6-0 No 31846 (83D Bude) at Halwill Junction on an up freight from Bude 11 July 1964. Freight facilities were withdrawn from this area 7 September 1964. A poster advertises Morecambe & Heysham. R.A. Lumber

LSWR set No 224 forms an Up train leaving Holsworthy circa 1895. The timber-built engine shed is to the left of the rear coach. Notice the stack of baskets on the Down platform. Author's collection

At Whitstone & Bridgerule 23 August 1960, T9 class 4-4-0 No 30715 with a Down train waits to cross an Up train. R.A.Lumber

Battle of Britain class Pacific No 34066 *Spitfire* collects the single line tablet at Ashwater while working the Up 'Atlantic Coast Express', 11 July 1964. *Spitfire* was involved in the Lewisham disaster 4 December 1957. R.A.Lumber

1966, while freight had been withdrawn two years earlier. Holsworthy Viaduct was the most significant engineering feature. Of nine 50ft spans, it had the honour of being the first large viaduct to be built in Britain.

Halwill Junction to Launceston

The fourth line to Halwill Junction was the North Cornwall Railway which received its Act 28 July 1884 to construct a line from Halwill to Padstow via Launceston. The line was opened to Launceston ceremonially on 20 July 1886 and to the public the following day. 1½ miles east of Launceston the line crossed Polston Bridge over the River Tamar and passed into Cornwall. The extension to Padstow, opened 27 March

A 3-car DMU working the 11.55 Halwill Junction to Wadebridge on 3 September 1966, calls at Tower Hill following the station's reduction to halt status. Only the former Up road is in use as the signal box, established in the office 28 March 1943, closed 7 November 1965. The original signal box, closed 15 June 1920, was at the far end of the Down platform.
R.A.Lumber

The Lynton & Barnstaple Railway seal.

1899, was leased by the LSWR which absorbed it in 1922. The branch was severely affected by road competition and closed 3 October 1966 throwing the 42 staff out of work.

The Lynton & Barnstaple Railway

Back in 1895 a four-horse coach covered the 18 miles between Barnstaple and Lynton in 2 hours 50 minutes. A modern railway was called for, but a standard gauge line over such hilly terrain would have been uneconomic. However, the narrow gauge with 1 ft 11½ in between the rails could follow the sharp contours and cost only a third of the price of a standard gauge line. The Act was passed on 27 June 1895, but the cost of blasting through unexpected rock bankrupted the contractor. The line opened ceremonially on 11 May 1898 and to the public on 16 May. Sir George Newnes who opened the line, told the *Railway Magazine* that 'I believe that Lynton has for some time enjoyed the distinction of being the only place in England extensively visited by tourists, despite the fact that it is twenty miles from any railway station...It has been the regular thing in July and August to see twenty or thirty coaches and *chars-a-bancs* from Ilfracombe crowd into Lynton between 11 and 12 o'clock in the morning.'

The Lynton & Barnstaple Railway (LBR) operated the first railway-owned bus feeder service in Great Britain.

From 30 May 1903 two 22-seat 16hp Milnes-Daimler buses linked Ilfracombe with Blackmoor station. When the police found them illegally 'speeding above 8 mph' the buses were sold to the GWR. In March 1923 the SR purchased the independent line. Despite improvements, the SR was unable to successfully compete with road transport, ticket sales falling from 72,000 in 1925 to 32,000 in 1934. In 1935 the choice had to be made between permanent way renewal or closure. The latter course was adopted.

Following the line's closure, Southern National buses were constructed to carry mail, milk churns and even sheep and goats. They covered the

The simple, yet attractive, Snapper Halt which opened February 1903. The view is towards Barnstaple. Author's collection

2-6-2T No 760 *Exe* at Woody Bay with a mixed train to Barnstaple. The boy in the cab is having a ride of some length because the chain is across the doorway. Lens of Sutton

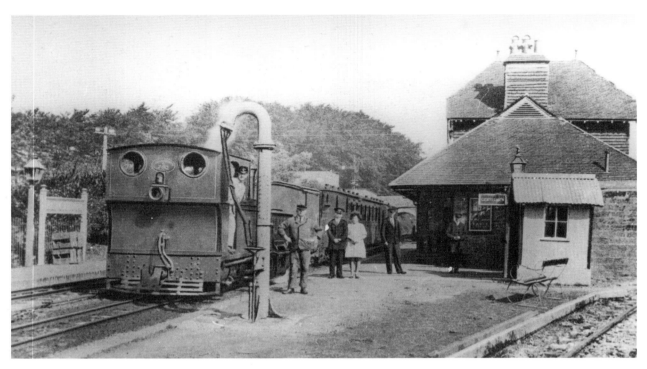

A Manning, Wardle 2-6-2T heading an Up train, takes water at Blackmoor Gate 1930. The water supply tank can be seen above the first coach. The train crew, one passenger and two porters, pose for this photograph. Author's collection

distance in 1 hour 35 minutes. Trains were allowed about 1½ hours for the 19 mile journey – quite good considering the fact that mixed trains were run involving shunting at several stations. Slow speed could be an advantage. One friend of the author's got off at a station to use the toilet and found the train had left before he could re-board. Undaunted, he ran after it and jumped on. People from South Wales could enjoy an excursion using a variety of transport: paddle steamer to Ilfracombe; standard gauge railway to Barnstaple Town; narrow gauge railway to Lynton; horse-drawn coach to Minehead or Ilfracombe and finally home to South Wales by paddle steamer. It is interesting that the line's five engines were all named after three-letter local rivers: Yeo, Exe, Taw, Lyn and Lew.

The LBR started at Barnstaple Town. Transfer between the gauges was simple – one just walked across the platform. Apart from Barnstaple,

2-6-2T No 760 *Exe* at Lynton prepares for departure to Barnstaple, 1929. C.T.Standfast

Standard and narrow gauge at Barnstaple Town 17 July 1935. N class 2-6-0 is on the train to Ilfracombe and 2-6-2T No 188 *Lew* on that to Lynton. S.W.Baker

platforms were low – only just raised above ground level. Chelfham Viaduct was the principal engineering feature, with eight 42ft spans 70ft high; it is now Grade II listed. Woody Bay station was at the line's summit 980ft above sea level. Lynton station, 750ft above sea level was carefully placed in order to be invisible from Lynton and Lynmouth and not spoil the scenery. However its situation, 250ft above the town could have been considered an error of judgement.

In August 1935 the SR issued a notice: Make sure of a trip this holiday over the Barnstaple and Lynton, through the beautiful scenery of the miniature alps of North Devon, along the edge of Exmoor. This line will be closed after September 29, 1935.

There was pathos on the day following closure when the stationmaster at Barnstaple laid on the narrow gauge track a wreath sent by Paymaster Captain Woolf, RN (retired) of Woody Bay. It bore a black-edged mourning card with the inscription: "To Barnstaple and Lynton Railway, with regret and sorrow from a constant user and admirer; 'Perchance it is not dead, but sleepeth' ". Much of the railway was auctioned on 13 November 1935 at the line's depot at Pilton, Barnstaple. Locomotives were sold for £34-£52 each; coaches for £10-£13 10s 0d and open wagons for £3 15s 0d.

Preservationist have always rued the fact that the line closed when it did. Had it been able to survive for a further fifteen years, it might have become the first British narrow gauge railway to be preserved as an entity. However not all is lost. The Lynton & Barnstaple Railway Association has purchased Woody Bay station, relaid the track southwards towards Parracombe and started running steam trains. On 27 May 2006 the first public train ran the mile to a temporary terminus at Killington Lane. Woody Bay station, like those at Blackmoor and Lynton, were built in the Nuremberg chalet style.

Bere Alston to Gunnislake

The branch began as the Callington & Calstock Railway which received its Act on 9 August 1869, opened its 3ft 6in gauge line to mineral traffic on 7 May 1872. This line was entirely in Cornwall.

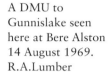

A DMU to Gunnislake seen here at Bere Alston 14 August 1969. R.A.Lumber

Ex-Plymouth, Devonport & South Western Junction Railway 0-6-2T as SR No E758 *Lord St Levan*, at Bere Alston with the 11.28am to Callington 31 March 1923. Notice that the coach is of the gated-stock type. Author's collection

When the Plymouth, Devonport & South Western Junction Railway (PDSWJR) opened from Lydford to Devonport on 2 June 1890, it was obvious that a line should be built to create a link between Gunnislake and the PDSWJR at Bere Alston. The Bere Alston & Calstock Light Railway obtained its Light Railway Order 13 July 1900. Further Orders granted extension of time and the authorised standard gauge. It opened 2 March 1908 with its own stud of locomotives, originally painted in blue livery, but changed to LSWR green about 1912. In 1922 it became part of the LSWR and was dieselised 4 September 1964. 7 November 1966 the branch was truncated beyond Callington and actually had no station in Devon. The line is now marketed as the Tamar Valley Line and offers a most scenic trip.

Callington trains were accommodated at the outer face of the Up platform at Bere Alston, but since the main line Bere Alston to Tavistock was closed 6 May 1968, today's trains use the former Down platform where they reverse. Leaving Bere Alston the line falls steeply round a tight curve. It appears as if it is going to cross the Tamar, but then swings northwards to offer a wonderful vista of the river winding below. Another sharp curve brings the line to the Grade II listed Calstock Viaduct. Consisting of 12 arches of 60ft span with a maximum height of 120ft, it crosses into Cornwall. The viaduct is constructed of massive concrete blocks each weighing at least a ton. Cast on site, they resemble stone.

Plymouth Friary to Turnchapel

The Plymouth & Dartmoor Railway Act of 2 August 1883 authorised a line from Laira station to Turnchapel on the southern side of the Cattewater. It opened to Pomphlett for goods traffic on 25 June 1888 and to passengers on

An H12 class steam railcar at Turnchapel circa 1905, view towards Plymouth. Author's collection

A 2-coach train for Friary at Turnchapel circa 1933 headed by 02 class 0-4-4T No 182. The compressed air cylinders on the running plate and the pump beside the smoke box, indicate that it has been fitted with motor train equipment for push-pull working. The train is of gated stock. Notice the disc and tail lamp. Lens of Sutton

5 September 1892 when Pomphlett station was renamed Plymstock. In the meantime a new Plymouth & Dartmoor Railway Act of 3 July 1891 revised powers for constructing the section to Turnchapel. The 94yd long Hooe Lake swing bridge was the most notable engineering feature. The line, worked by the LSWR from Friary station, opened 1 January 1897.

As there was an attractive beach near Turnchapel station, it saw use by many trippers. Turnchapel was the LSWR's southernmost station. On this branch the first LSWR steam rail motor service in the south west was inaugurated on 10 October 1904. The self-contained vehicle did not prove a success and was replaced by a conventional locomotive and push-pull coaches. To economise on station staff, tickets were issued by a conductor. As goods trains shunted the timber yard at Oreston, for safety, locomotives were required to be fitted with spark arresters.

Owing to a post-WW2 fuel crisis, the branch was temporarily closed to passengers January to July 1951 and permanently on 10 September 1951. An unusual competitor was the ferry, as steamers only needed to travel half the distance. The line south of Plymstock closed completely 2 October 1961.

The Cattewater, Friary, Stonehouse Road & Sutton Harbour Branches

On 2 July 1821 the Plymouth & Dartmoor Railway Act authorised an extension from Laira to Cattedown and Sutton Pool. A further Act of 19 July 1875 authorised the Plymouth & Dartmoor Railway to construct a branch to Cattewater. This was purchased by the LSWR in 1909. The Friary marshalling yard gained importance following the closure of the Tavistock Junction yard 4 January 1971. However Friary subsequently closed and track cut back to the station throat. The LSWR's single track branch to Sutton Harbour curved away southwards just east of Friary station. It then entered a cutting and tunnel, emerging to pass over Sutton Road level crossing.

8 Independent Lines & Industrial Branches

The Bideford, Westward Ho! & Appledore Railway

The Bideford & Westward Ho! Railway was probably the only railway in the world to have an exclamation mark in its title. The reason was that the settlement of Westward Ho! Took its name from Charles Kingsley's novel. Even before the novel was published, the Northam Burrows Hotel & Villa Company had commenced building operations on the sea front, so when the

149

A Bideford &
Westward Ho!
Railway 2-4-0T
and coaches at
Appledore. The
advertisement is for
'Prior, decorator'.
Author's collection

novel was published, the opportunity to name the new community after the book was too good to miss.

The line was built under an Act of 21 May 1886 and while still under construction, in 1900 became a subsidiary of British Electric Traction, a company which owned an extensive range of electric street tramways.

The line between Bideford Quay and Northam opened 18 May 1901 with steam traction. An unusual clause in the timetable stated that: 'The published timetables are only intended to fix the time before which the trains will not start, and the company do not undertake that the trains shall start or arrive at the times specified in the tables'.

The three 2-4-2 tank engines had side plates covering the wheels and motion in order to carry out road working at Bideford Quay. They hauled American-type coaches with end balconies. Lit by acetylene gas, they were unusual in having a single central buffer – common on the narrow gauge, but probably unique on British standard gauge. Some coaches had double-faced clocks displayed inside near the roof. The first class compartments were upholstered in leather. Rolling stock consisted of 6 coaches, one brake van and 8 goods vehicles. Due to paucity of traffic, most trains consisted of just a single coach and freight traffic was negligible. The booking office and waiting room at Bideford Quay were in the ground floor of 20 The Quay, though in fine weather potential passengers sat outside on benches. When travelling on the street section along the quay, the fireman stood on the front of the engine ringing a warning bell. In Bideford streets the flat-bottomed rail was enclosed in brick. Due to its tramway character it made 12 stops in 7 miles. The line was extended to Appledore on 1 May 1908. Through bookings could be made to and from the LSWR. In 1917 the fare was 8d return

and books of 10 tickets could be purchased for 3s 4d. The purchaser of a normal return ticket was entitled to a discount if he used the Great Nassau Baths at Bideford.

Apart from the exclamation mark curiosity, a concert hall was adjacent to Westward Ho! station where entertainments such as black minstrels took place. Combined rail and admission tickets were issued.

During WW1 the government requisitioned locomotives and rails for the war effort so the last trains ran on 28 March 1917. As the line was completely independent of the rest of the British railway system, the three locomotives were removed by temporary track being laid over Bideford Bridge to give access to the LSWR.

A 2-4-0T being taken across Bideford Bridge on a specially laid track following closure of the Bideford & Westward Ho! Railway in 1917. Author's collection

Industrial Branches

The Westleigh Tramway

Westleigh Quarries near Burlescombe owned a ¾ mile long 3ft gauge tramway to link with the B&E at Burlescombe. Opened 12 January 1875 it was worked by the B&E and meant that from this date the B&E operated trains on three gauges: narrow, standard and broad. As the B&E possessed no 3ft gauge locomotives, two 0-4-0WTs were specially built at the B&E's works at Bristol. Following the amalgamation of the B&E with the GWR in 1876, GWR brass number plates had to be fixed to the rear of the cab as there was no suitable surface for the usual side position. The GWR lease expired about

The Westleigh
Tramway in 1898:
the 3ft gauge B&E
0-4-0WT on the
timber viaduct with
a Manning Wardle
0-6-0ST below.
Camas UK Ltd

The Westleigh
Tramway bridge
over the Grand
Western Canal
right, and its
towpath, left;
viewed on 31 May
1994. Author

1898 and the quarry company converted the line to standard gauge and worked the line itself.

The standard gauge track was Vignoles rail spiked directly to the sleepers; interestingly sidings and points were of bridge rail as used on many broad gauge lines. These remained until rail traffic ceased about 1950. In 1977 some of this bridge rail, by that date extremely rare except in very short lengths, still lay in situ. It was recovered and relaid by the Great Western Society at Didcot to form its very interesting example of a mixed gauge line.

The Exeter City Basin Branch

The South Devon Railway Act of 5 July 1865 granted powers for building the 750yd long Exeter City basin line. It opened on the broad gauge 17 June 1867. In February 1870 it was converted to mixed gauge and by the autumn of 1870 the main Down line from St David's to City Basin Junction was also converted to mixed gauge. The standard gauge remained unused until 20 March 1871 when the LSWR made a connection.

A train to and from the City Basin was a sight to behold. If it consisted of wagons of both gauges, a rake of broad gauge wagons was linked with its standard gauge counterpart by a match truck with buffers wide enough for both gauges. The coupling chain slid on a transverse bar. The branch eventually closed to public traffic in September 1965 becoming just a private siding.

The Teignmouth Quay Branch

About 1850 a broad gauge siding served the Old Quay ¼ mile west of Teignmouth station. Locomotives were not permitted beyond the Stop Board just inside the quay gates, so propulsion was by horses. Circa 1924 a petrol driven tractor superseded the horses, but was not an outstanding success. About 1931 a Sentinel steam tractor fitted with timber baulks for buffers, worked successfully until 1963 when an agricultural diesel tractor, also fitted with timber baulks, took over until closure 2 December 1967 with the opening of Exmouth Junction Coal Concentration Depot.

The Totnes Quay Branch

The Totnes Quay branch, ¾ mile in length, opened 10 November 1873 as part of the Buckfastleigh, Totnes & South Devon Railway. It served Totnes Market, South Devon Farmers, Symond's Cyder and the quay itself where timber was imported. Most of the line could be locomotive worked, but from just short of the A385 Totnes to Paignton road level crossing, horse traction was used until 1950 when replaced by an agricultural tractor fitted with a front buffer plate. The branch closed 7 December 1969.

The Lee Moor Tramway

The Lee Moor Tramway opened an 8½ mile long line in September 1854, but closed it on 4 October 1854 after an accident caused by poor workmanship. It re-opened on 29 September 1858. It was 4ft 6in gauge with horse haulage. It had two rope-worked balanced inclines: at Cann Wood and Torycombe. In due course the 2½ mile length from Cann Wood to Torycombe was locomotive-worked, but the other lengths remained horse-worked. Surprisingly horses continued to haul wagons occasionally over the Plymouth to Exeter main line crossing at Laira until about 1950. This level crossing over the main line was lifted in October 1960. In 1964 the Peckett locomotives and engine shed at Torycombe were acquired for preservation.

Devon Great Consols Limited, Tavistock

From 1858 Devon Great Consols Limited, which mined copper and arsenic, operated a locomotive-worked 4½ mile long standard gauge line east of the Tamar about a mile north of Gunnislake, to give access to Morwellham Quay. The final section to the quay was down a self-acting incline. The line closed in December 1901.

The Redlake Tramway

The Redlake Tramway was a 3ft gauge line which opened 11 September 1911 by the China Clay Corporation. That company owned three engines for the 3ft and one for the 2ft gauge used on higher level workings. Its main line linked the china clay deposits at Redlake Marshes with the GWR. In the 7½ miles of route the line rose over 1,000ft. A short cable-operated incline was situated where the GWR laid a transfer siding just east of Ivybridge.

The china clay was removed by pipeline, but the railway was used in the morning for conveying both the workmen, and coal for the pumping engine, to the china clay quarry, Redlake. In the evening it returned with the workmen and sand for building or use as a fertiliser. The three passenger coaches, described by H.G. Kendall in the *Railway Magazine* of June 1952 as being 'vaguely reminiscent of a mobile hen house', could carry a maximum of 30 passengers. Other rolling stock comprised 12 5-ton coal wagons and 12 5-ton sand trucks. Wagons were unbraked and were fitted with the usual narrow gauge centre buffer-coupling. The tramway and works closed in 1932 and the track lifted the following year.

The Devonport Dockyard Railway

The Royal Naval Dockyards at Devonport covered an area of almost 300 acres. From 1867 it was served by a horse-worked standard gauge railway, but two years later an Aveling & Porter geared 0-4-0T was used. Normal 0-4-0STs were used from 1898. These were replaced by 4-wheeled diesel-mechanical locomotives in 1955, though four steam engines lasted until passenger services were withdrawn 16 May 1966. The four-wheeled passenger coaches constructed in the dockyard workshops, were unusual in that they catered for no less than six classes: Principal Dockyard Officers; Superior and Commissioned Officers; Subordinate Officers; Chief Petty Officers and Chargemen; Recorders and Petty Officers; and Workmen and Ratings. Only the first three classes enjoyed padded seats and lighting. Locomotive No 1 hauled the coach containing Edward VII and Queen

Alexandra when they visited the dockyard in March 1902. No 1 carried the Royal coat-of-arms in brass and this was never removed.

At the time of writing the connection with the main line remains, but is out of use.

Devonport Dockyard 0-4-0ST No 7 built by Hawthorn, Leslie, hauling a passenger train. It bears the Royal coat of arms. Author's collection

9 **An Overview**

What have railways done for Devon? Before the coming of the railways life in the county moved at a slow pace – even getting from one side of Devon to the other was impossible in a day except on a very few stage-coach routes. For many, travel was unnecessary because they lived and worked within walking distance of their homes. Agriculture was mostly dairying, the climate favouring meadows, and butter and cheese stayed fresh long enough to travel to market. Oats were important as horse feed for coaching inns. The introduction of railways caused a dramatic change to the lives of some innkeepers and farmers: innkeepers on once busy road lost their trade, and farmers had to change to growing other crops.

The railway station developed as a social centre with shops or stalls starting up nearby, assured of regular trade. The stationmaster was a man of importance almost ranking with the doctor, rector or school headmaster. A good stationmaster made it his job to keep in touch with local developments, for he was responsible for bringing business to his railway. In the 19th century a town with a railway thrived, a town without a railway tended to become a backwater.

The railway offered a greater variety of employment than had been available in a district before its arrival. To progress through the railway ranks one needed to move, no longer staying in the same house or even in the same native village. Sometimes only a day's notice was given to report to another station.

The coming of the railway led to a greater use of coal for cooking and heating than hitherto, for unless home was near a waterway or the sea, transportation of coal was expensive and wood proved a cheaper fuel. A greater variety of building material could be used, not just local stone or brick, but different materials brought cheaply from a distance such as slates and tiles which rendered thatch out of date.

With cheap transport, industry could develop: a workshop need no longer just supply the district, but could become a factory supplying the whole country or even the whole world. The railway enabled the cottager's wife to travel to a larger market town where she could receive a better price for her butter, cheese and eggs, more than offsetting the cost of her ticket.

Railways affected diet. No longer did one have to rely on what was grown in one's garden or grown locally. Food could be transported cheaply from, or to other parts of the country. Cattle, fish and rabbits were sent from Devon, while such things as oranges and bananas could be imported and distributed.

The Workmen's Early Morning Return enabled people to travel cheaply by rail as long as they reached their destination by 8.00am. That time limit was imposed to prevent white collar workers who were better paid and could afford the full price, from taking advantage of cheap fares.

Railways enabled the many seaside resorts in Devon to grow and be accessible to the many, unlike the select watering places available to the rich few. This development led to further job opportunities such as being a full, or part-time boarding house keeper. Ancillary industries followed – catering and retailing to fulfil the need of the tourist. Seaside shops received many of their goods by rail and the railway's horse-drawn cart or motor lorry made a daily delivery. Apart from overnight stays, the resorts could be visited cheaply by day return excursion trains.

Railways played vital part in the war effort in two World Wars: they brought children to safe areas from cities likely to be bombed and carried troops to training camps in the county.

How has passenger transport changed between 1850 and 2010? In 1850, as today, not all Devon settlements were served by rail, and road transport was essential for at least part of the journey. By 1910 many settlements were served by rail, a walk of up to two miles to a station being thought not unreasonable. Railways enabled people to travel across the county, perhaps with the fuss of changing trains at junctions. There was little alternative to rail travel in 1910, but today road travel from one part of the county to another is probably more convenient than rail unless other factors come into the equation: crowded roads, parking problems, or lack of driving ability. For longer distances, internal air travel now competes with long distance railway journeys. Because of the closure of local stations, except in the Exeter and Plymouth areas, short distance rail commuter traffic is less common than formerly. In 2010 rail travel comes into its own for long distances; it is more restful for the traveller and better for the environment.

Business and holiday travel were present in 1850 and 2010 but special excursion traffic has all but disappeared. Today's trains are of fixed length and inflexible. Until about forty years ago, a sudden influx of traffic would produce one or several extra coaches or even a duplicate train to fulfil the need. Today, services are run with the minimum number of vehicles to maximise the investment and overcrowding can be a serious complaint.

Rail freight has changed. In 1850 railways were the common carrier and would transport any item from a small parcel to an elephant, or tons of coal. In 2010 railways only deal with bulk items such as clay or stone. A freight train is a relatively rare sight in 2010; the line-side watcher in 1850 or 1910 would have seen as many freight as passenger trains.

And what of the future for the railways of Devon? Here the author might be permitted to indulge his personal vision. I would like to see more encouragement to use the train, rather than the car, for longer journeys. Free station parking would help, perhaps not in larger towns where people should be encouraged to use the bus to reach the station, but certainly at more rural stations. I would like to see plenty of space on trains, rather than passengers packed in airline style. Space is limited in a car and space could pull people from the car into the train. I don't anticipate many more stations being re-opened because each stop delays a train and if a train is slow, people will not use it because it would be quicker to go by road. And as for commercial use, I would like to see the loads of long-distance lorries carried by rail, road being used only for collection and local distribution. That would benefit the environment.

Re-opening the line from Bere Alston to Tavistock seems likely. West Devon Borough Council has voted in favour of outline plans to build 750 houses at Tavistock, including a £18.5m rail link to offset the increase in traffic. When this work is carried out a continuation to Meldon would offer an alternative to the Teignmouth – Dawlish length which has always been liable to damage. The Association of Train Operating Companies' report 'Connecting Communities' recommends that the Churston to Brixham branch be re-opened.

Doubling the track from Exeter to Chard Junction would improve the punctuality of train services on that line. At the time of writing the loop is being restored at Axminster to permit an hourly service Waterloo to Exeter Central and an intermediate shuttle service to operate between Exeter and Axminster. This will bring a highly intensive use of the 14 miles of single track Honiton to Pinhoe. An essential time table improvement required, is a better connection at Exeter St David's between Barnstaple line trains and those to Waterloo.

The scenic potential of the county's branch lines is not sufficiently exploited – much more could be made of the scenic delights of the line between Dawlish-Teignmouth, Topsham-Exmouth and Plymouth-Calstock.

Through the efforts of preservation societies, localities are realising the economic benefits that a railway can bring to communities. Visitors to preserved railways bring trade to that area when they use shops, hotels, camp-sites and eating places. Although I feel that saturation point has been reached and that there could be insufficient enthusiasts to run some lines in the future, I would like to see the superb Lynton & Barnstaple Railway completely re-opened. I would also like to see a short length of the Haytor Tramway fully restored with a horse drawn wagon offering rides at weekends and holiday periods. What a splendid opportunity for railway enthusiasts and equestrian lovers to unite.

And what of those railways closed and not brought back into use? A significant number of them, their formations almost forgotten except perhaps for use as unofficial footpaths, are now becoming official paths and cycle ways offering gentle routes through the heart of the countryside and hopefully away from the sound of road transport.

Suggested Further Reading

Antell, R., *Southern Country Stations: 1 London & South Western Railway* (Ian Allan, 1984)

Anthony, G.H., revised Jenkins, S.C, *The Launceston Branch* (Oakwood Press,1997)

Austin, S., *From the Footplate of the Atlantic Coast Express* (Ian Allan, 1989)

Bastin, C.H., *The Tiverton Branch & the Hemyock Branch* (Author,1989)

Bastin, C.H., *The Exmouth, Sidmouth & Budleigh Salterton Branch Lines* (Author, 1990)

Beck, K. & Copsey, J., *The Great Western in South Devon* (Wild Swan, 1990)

Bennett, A., *Southern Holiday Lines in North Cornwall & West Devon* (Runpast Publishing, 1995)

Bolger, P., *BR Steam Motive Power Depots SR* (Ian Allan, 1983)

Body, G., *Railways of the Western Region* (Patrick Stephens, 1983)

Body, G., *Railways of the Southern Region* (Patrick Stephens, 1984)

Catchpole, L.T., *The Lynton & Barnstaple Railway* (Oakwood Press, 1988)

Clarke, R.H., *An Historical Survey of Selected Great Western Railway Stations, Layouts and Illustrations* (Oxford Publishing Co, volume 1 1976, volume 2 1979, volume 3 1981)

Clarke, W.G., *Oh, Mr Porter!* [Budleigh Salterton branch] (Granary Press,1983)

Clinker, C.R., *Register of Closed Passenger Stations and Goods Depots 1830-1977* (Avon Anglia,1978)

Cooke, R.A., *Track Layout Diagrams of the GWR and BR WR* (Author, Part 12,1984; Part 14, 1984; Part 15 1986)

Crombleholme, R., Gibson, B., Stuckey, D. & Whetmath, C.F.D., *Callington Railways* (Forge Books, 1985)

Crombleholme, R., Stuckey, D. & Whetmath, C.F.D., *The Culm Valley Light Railway* (Branch Line Handbooks, 1964)

Ellis, H., *The South Western Railway* (Allen & Unwin, 1956)

Faulkner, J.N. & Williams, R.A., *The LSWR in the Twentieth Century* (David & Charles, 1988)

Gosling, E. & Clement, M., *Devon Railways* (Sutton Publishing, 1997)

Gregory, R.H., *The South Devon Railway* (Oakwood Press, 1982)

Hall, J., *Railway Landmarks in Devon* (David & Charles, 1982)

Harris, H., *The Haytor Granite Tramway & Stover Canal* (Peninsula Press, 1994)

Hateley, R., *Industrial Railways of South West England* (Industrial Railway Society, 1977)

Hawkins, C. & Reeve, G., *An Historical Survey of Southern Sheds* (Oxford Publishing Co, 1979)

Hawkins, C. & Reeve, G., *London & South Western Engine Sheds* (Irwell Press, 1990)

Hudson, D., *The Lynton & Barnstaple Railway Anthology* (Oakwood Press, 1995)

Jenkins, S.C., & Pomroy, L.J., *The Moretonhampstead & South Devon Railway* (Oakwood Press, 1989)

Karau, P., *Great Western Branch Line Termini Volume 2* (Oxford Publishing Co, 1978)

Kay, P., *Exeter to Newton Abbot* (Platform 5, 1993)

Lyons, E., *An Historical Survey of Great Western Engine Sheds 1947* (Oxford Publishing Co 1974)

MacDermot, E. T., revised Clinker, C.R, *History of the Great Western Railway, Volumes 1 & 2* (Ian Allan, 1964)

Madge, R., *Railways Round Exmoor* (Exmoor Press, 1971)

Maggs, C.G., *The Barnstaple & Ilfracombe Railway* (Oakwood Press, 1988)

Maggs, C.G., *The Seaton Branch & Seaton Tramway* (Oakwood Press, 1992)

Maggs, C.G., *The Sidmouth & Budleigh Salterton Branches* (Oakwood Press, 1996)

Maggs, C.G., *The Exeter & Exmouth Railway* (Oakwood Press 1997)

Maggs, C.G., *The Culm Valley Light Railway* (Oakwood Press, 2006)

Maggs, C.G., *Branch Lines of Devon: Exeter & South, Central & East Devon* (Alan Sutton, 1995)

Maggs, C.G., *Branch Lines of Devon: Plymouth, West & North Devon* (Alan Sutton,1995)

Maggs, C.G., *GWR Principal Stations* (Ian Allan, 1987)

Maggs, C.G., *Rail Centres: Exeter* (Ian Allan, 1985)

Maggs, C.G., *Colin Maggs's West of England* (Alan Sutton, 1998)

Maggs, C.G., *The Taunton to Barnstaple Line* (Oakwood Press, 1980)

Maggs, C.G. & Paye, P., *The Sidmouth, Seaton & Lyme Regis Branches* (Oakwood Press, 1977)

Marshall, C.F.D., revised Kidner, R.W., *History of the Southern Railway* (Ian Allan, 1963)

Messenger, M., *The Culm Valley Light Railway* (Twelveheads Press, 1993)

Mitchell, V. & Smith, K., Middleton Press
Branch Line to Ashburton, 1997
Branch Line to Bude, 1994
Branch Lines to Exmouth, 1992
Branch Line to Ilfracombe, 1993
Branch Line to Kingswear, 1998
Branch Lines to Launceston and Princetown, 1998
Branch Line to Lyme Regis, 1987
Branch Line to Lynton, 1992
Branch Line to Moretonhampstead, 1998
Branch Line to Padstow, 1995
Branch Lines around Plymouth, 1997
Branch Lines to Seaton and Sidmouth, 1991
Branch Lines around Tiverton, 2001
Branch Lines to Torrington, 1994
Exeter to Barnstaple, 1993
Exeter to Newton Abbot,2000
Exeter to Tavistock, 1996
Newton Abbot to Plymouth, 2001
Plymouth to St Austell, 2001
Taunton to Barnstaple, 1995
Taunton to Exeter,2002
Yeovil to Exeter, 1991

Nicholas, J., *The Ilfracombe Line* (Irwell Press, 1998)

Nicholas, J., *The North Devon Line,* (Oxford Publishing Co, 1992)

Nicholas, J., *Lines to Torrington* (Oxford Publishing Co, 1984)

Nicholas, J. & Reeve, G., *Main Line to the West Part 3* (Irwell Press, 2009)

Oakley, M., *Devon Railway Stations* (Dovecote Press, 2007)

Owen, J., *The Exe Valley Railway* (Kingfisher, 1985)

Phillips, D. & Pryer, G., *The Salisbury to Exeter Line* (Oxford Publishing Co, 1997)

Phillips, D. & Pryer, G., *From Salisbury to Exeter: The Branch Lines* (Oxford Publishing Co, 2000)

Pomroy, L.W, *The Teign Valley Line* (Oxford Publishing Co, 1984)

Popplewell, C., *A Gazetteer of the Railway Contractors & Engineers of the West Country* (Melledgen Press, 1983)

Potts, C.R., *The Brixham Branch* (Oakwood Press, 1986)

Potts, C. R., *An Historical Survey of Selected Great Western Railway Stations, Layouts and Illustrations* (Oxford Publishing Co, Volume 4, 1985)

Potts, C.R., *The Newton Abbot to Kingswear Railway* (Oakwood Press, 1988)

Powell, A., *Feniton & the Railway* (Author, 1993)

Pryer, G.A., *Track Layout Diagrams of the Southern Railway & BR SR, Sections 5 & 6* (R.A. Cooke, 1982, 1983)

Robertson, K., *Great Western Halts* Volume 1 (Irwell Press, 1990); Volume 2 (KBB Publications, 2002)

Rose, E.J., *The Axminster to Lyme Regis Railway* (Kingfisher, 1982)

Sekon, G.A., *The London & South Western Railway* (Avon Anglia [reprint] 1989)

Semmens, P., *The Withered Arm* (Ian Allan, 1988)

Smith, M., *The Railways of Devon* (Ian Allan, 1993)

Smith, M., *An Illustrated History of Exmoor's Railways* (Irwell Press, 1995)

Smith, M. & Reeve, G., *From Devon to Dorset. The Story of the Lyme Regis Branch* (Irwell Press,2003)

Swift, A., *Devon Railway Stations: GWR* (Reflections of a Bygone Age, 2001)

Swift, A., *Devon Railway Stations: SR* (Reflections of a Bygone Age, 2001)

Thomas, D. St J., *Regional History of the Railways of Great Britain, Volume 1, The West Country* (David & Charles, 1981)

Whetmath, C.F.D. & Stuckey, D., *The North Devon & Cornwall Light Railway* (Forge Books, 1980)

Williams, K. & Reynolds, D., *The Kingsbridge Branch* (Oakwood Press, 1997)

Williams, R.A., *The London & South Western Railway Volumes 1 & 2* (David & Charles 1968; 1973)

Worth, R.H., *Early Western Railroads* (Avon Anglia, no date)

Wroe, D.J., *The Atlantic Coast Express* (Waterfront Publications, 1995)

Wroe, D.J., *The North Cornwall Railway* (Irwell Press, 1995)